AF594406

To everyone who has
ever sought solace
in the quietness
of plants.

A practical guide to winning over your indoor plants

GREEN THUMB

Craig Miller-Randle

plum. Pan Macmillan Australia

INTRODUCTION

When I was only knee high, my father built a small greenhouse at the back of our home and filled it with hanging orchids and other tropical plants. Looking back now, it occurs to me that my dad would only have been in his early twenties and, like me, he was a true plant nerd early in life! I was fascinated by the plants as well as the humid, jungle-like atmosphere of the greenhouse; the scent of the flowers and the beauty of the plants were wondrous, like the tropical butterflies and iridescent beetles I had seen at the museum and become fascinated by. The plants in Dad's greenhouse hung there perfectly, like artworks in a gallery – however, unlike paintings, I could actually grow and nurture these natural works of art myself. That sense of wonder has never left me and it still underpins much of my passion for collecting, growing and styling plants indoors.

Caving to the insistent demands of my four-year-old self, my father gave me my own orchid, a *Cattleya*, the kind with the big, showy flowers that women used to pin on their dresses for an evening out. In grey lead pencil he wrote 'Craig's Orchid' on the terracotta pot. I cared for that plant until my forties, when it got lost in the flurry of one of life's unplanned events. I still miss it and wish I had looked after it with more care.

When I was six years old, we moved into a large Edwardian home on a huge block of land with upwards of 25 fruit trees. My grandmother, Mimi, as we called her ('no one is calling *me* Grandma'), lived behind us in a rather glam granny flat and was an avid gardener – I'm sure my father inherited his leaning towards all things botanical from her. She also had her own garden, which was filled with bamboos, camellias and wisteria-covered trees, as well as ivy, gardenias and begonias, and each year a new display of garish but glorious annuals.

My darling Mimi decided to encourage my passion by giving me my very own patch of earth in her garden; it was about a square metre and halfway down the side of her house in the shade. She told me the patch was mine to do with whatever I wanted. I felt so excited and full of hope at the prospect of what I could grow. Having responsibility for my own garden made me feel like an adult, and I set about not only cultivating my plot but also taking over her garden – what a brat!

I probably went too far; I was always experimenting with ways of growing things and I remember cutting most of the leaves off her beloved iron cross begonia (*Begonia masoniana*). I left two leaves on the plant so as to not attract attention, and then cut the prunings into pieces, each containing a vein. I planted the cuttings into numerous pots and hid them in another part of the garden, in the hope of presenting her with lots of new plants when they took off. Unfortunately, when she found a pot of nearly leafless stems sitting on her garden table – where once had sat her pride and joy – she didn't share my vision. I think she questioned whether giving me free rein over her paradise was a good idea until a year later, when I did in fact present her with about twenty small but perfectly formed begonias. All she could say with a look of joyful surprise was 'Did *you* do that?'. Okay, this story has a happy ending but to any young ones reading this, I emphasise – do not try this at home! At least not without asking your granny first, anyway!

Through my teen years, plants remained ever present. I never stopped growing them, observing them and learning the best ways to care for them. I read books about plants voraciously and by the time I was fifteen I knew almost every indoor plant by its scientific name. Around the same age, my father helped me build a greenhouse (well, I helped him build one!), where I cultivated orchids and other tropical plants. I also grew African violets and angel wing caladiums in my bedroom, under fluorescent grow lights. I had about 40 African violets on pebble-filled trays to boost humidity. It was quite difficult to grow that many African violets in a room carpeted in cream shagpile, and while the violets were thriving, the carpet under the trays was turning black and falling apart … oops! I was too busy getting amazing results with my violets to notice things like carpet.

After high school, I began studying horticulture, but soon found that despite my passion for plants, the world of horticulture as it was back then wasn't a great fit for me, stifling my creativity rather than nurturing it. I took up a job in a nursery and flower shop and ended up becoming the manager. I worked there for a few years, learning how to arrange flowers, buying and selling plants and honing my creative skills doing shop displays.

Later, I moved to a much larger nursery that specialised in ferns, carnivorous plants and orchids, where I dealt with customers and worked in the production nursery. We had our own wire workshop and sold hanging baskets, trellises and trainers used for topiaries and climbing plants. I'd been there for a couple of years when I noticed a rocket-shaped wire plant trainer. I had moved into a new apartment and needed some lamps, and it occurred to me that I could use this shape to make one. I asked the man who welded them to fasten a washer into the trainer to fit a lamp holder and light bulb, then I covered the frame in bright red Japanese mulberry paper to create a 1.5 m tall rocket-shaped lamp. I'd only had it a short time before a friend wanted to buy it. He owned a furniture store and the lamp sold within a day. 'Twelve more, please', was his next request, and before I knew it I had a thriving business selling handmade lamps to shops all over Melbourne.

That was the start of my company, MRD Home. The business grew; I designed new lamps and then whole ranges of lamps, travelled overseas to have my products manufactured, and soon added decorator accessories and textiles, followed by furniture. Through MRD Home, I have travelled many times to Bali, where I now have my own place and garden, and spend part of each year. All of those lush tropical plants and indoor–outdoor spaces have proven to be a boon for my plant collecting and styling.

I started my Instagram account a few years ago to share pictures of my obsession with plants, design and interiors, and after a few months I started to receive lots of messages from new followers who were plant lovers. It seems that indoor plants were having a resurgence in popularity. What joy for an old plant hermit, to suddenly realise that he's not the only person interested in filling his home with living greenery and making it look great to boot!

A little over 18 months later, I was contacted by the team at ABC's *Gardening Australia* and asked to present a six-segment special on indoor plants, which was shot in my Melbourne home. I was thrilled to have the chance to reach a wider audience and now I have an overwhelming desire to share what I know about plants with as many people as I can.

Tending to and caring for plants rewards me with feelings of satisfaction, excitement and joy that are hard to match. The sense of wellbeing and contentment that we feel from living with plants has only recently started to be appreciated by the scientific community, with a number of studies finding what we indoor gardeners have always known. There are lasting benefits to allowing nature into our living spaces: like the fact that having three or more medium-sized plants in a room brings about feelings of relaxation and positivity, as well as increasing focus and clarity. A recent study found that while a single plant offers little benefit to wellbeing, when you create a 'look' in your space with several plants your wellbeing starts to increase significantly. There is a direct correlation between the number and variety of plants and the improvement in mood and sense of relaxation. And it turns out our indoor beauties can also affect the air we breathe – even just three or four medium-sized plants can improve the air quality in your home.

I've collected lots of different plants over the years: orchids, cacti and succulents, carnivorous plants, African violets, bromeliads, aroids ... you name it, I've grown it! I didn't always have great success to start with; in fact, I would often quickly kill plants in my enthusiasm to care for them 'properly', only to learn later that I had done the exact opposite. Case in point, my first angel wings caladium: I stuck it in a fish-tank terrarium and heated it to 35°C, keeping it constantly wet with no air circulation because I figured that's as close to a jungle as I could get ... bye-bye plant. The constantly wet soil on its own would have been enough to kill it, let alone the lack of fresh air.

My failures led me to the most important piece of 'plantelligence' I have learned so far: no one is born with a green thumb, but with access to the right information, anyone can develop one! This is a deceptively simple idea but it encapsulates the true secret of plant-care mastery: practice and perseverance, combined with the relevant facts. You may think you're a born plant killer with plant triple-zero on speed dial, but with my support and some simple techniques, you can grow lush, envy-worthy specimens to fill any room of your home.

The advice in this book is a distillation of decades of experience, and it also contains all that I've learned from engaging with you, the people who love plants. I have received tens of thousands of messages and questions from followers on Instagram, asking about all types of plants and aspects of plant care, and it's put me in a unique position to know what your key concerns and problem areas are.

I'm going to show you how to make potting mixes that will yield results fast – just adding one or two ingredients to a basic potting mix can make such a difference. I'll simplify how to choose the right position for your plants so they won't feel like they've left the jungle, and also shed light on the topic that makes many a plant lover shudder … watering. After we've covered the basics, I'll share my styling tools of the trade to help you create gorgeous vistas of greenery. Of course, life is not always rosy in the indoor garden: pests and problems are inevitable, but there's a solution to each one and I'll help you to treat pests and diseases before they have a chance to do any damage.

Maybe you're at the beginning of your love affair with indoor plants, or perhaps you already have a home full of plant pets. Whatever your situation, my hope is that this book will help you select, care for and style your plants with a sense of fun and reward. I want to share my passion and be a kind of mentor, someone who comes up with the information you need when you need it! I wish you much success and may your thumbs become greener with each passing season.

A NOTE ON PLANT NAMES AND THE A–Z OF INDOOR PLANTS

Common names for indoor plants are as many and varied as the plants themselves, and are often unique to countries or regions. Some are commercial names dreamed up to help sell a plant, while others are colloquial and have become accepted after years of usage. *Epipremnum aureum* 'Snow Queen', for example, is known as 'Pothos N'joy' in the USA. Throughout this book I've chosen common names that are used in the Australasian region whenever possible.

Scientific names can be complex and are fluid, meaning that they change as botanists discover new genetic links between plants and decide that they belong in a different genus or the species is incorrect. Modern advances in DNA science have increased this phenomenon over recent years. Wherever possible I have used scientific names that are considered correct at the time of writing. For example, many *Sansevieria* or snake plants have been reclassified as *Dracaena*, and most *Calathea* or prayer plants have become *Goeppertia*, so I have used these. It's important not to stress too much over the common name or scientific name of an indoor plant – unless you're selling that plant for a lot of money. Most of us mispronounce the botanical names anyway!

The A–Z of indoor plants is not an exhaustive list of the most popular or readily available plants, although there are a lot of those in there. It's a list of my favourite plants that I think you'll enjoy growing. Many people ask me where I buy my plants from – I source them from a wide variety of places, including small plant shops, chain stores, nurseries, hardware store garden centres, eBay and even Instagram and Facebook.

Finally, you may notice that in the care requirements listed for each plant in the A–Z, there is sometimes more than one category chosen for light, water, temperature or soil. For example, a plant may be listed as suited to direct morning to bright filtered light, or cool to warm temperatures. This is because that plant will tolerate a broader range of conditions than simply what is optimal and it's important to know so that you can have more options when positioning and caring for it. However, the chapters dealing specifically with light, water and soil are generally more detailed, and most listed plants are assigned to the category that is optimal for each plant to do its absolute best.

A–Z OF INDOOR PLANTS

African violet

Saintpaulia ionantha

These plants are coming back into fashion again, which I love because I had a collection of around 40 when I was a teenager. I still think they are wonderful, with their clusters of jewel-like flowers sitting neatly on top of their compact, perfectly rosetted leaves. Bright filtered light is the key to good form and flowering. They can be finnicky when it comes to watering needs, preferring to be moist but not wet; water them under the leaves using a watering can with a narrow spout, as their leaves are prone to marking and fungal infections if they're regularly wet.

Light: Bright filtered

Water: Moderate

Soil: Jungle mix

Temperature: Warm

Air plant

Left: *Tillandsia stricta*
Right: *T. capitata*

Plants with virtually no roots come in handy for interior use because they're free agents, so to speak: they don't need soil and they can sit in or on virtually any vessel. Pop them on top of narrow-necked vases, in bowls and inside glass containers – your imagination is the only limit here. Most are hardy down to 16°C, but are happier around 18–28°C. They are forgiving of low water, but don't let them dry out for more than a couple of weeks at a time. In summer they like watering more frequently. There are lots of different sizes, shapes and forms to choose from, so go ahead and have fun with air plants!

Light: Bright filtered to medium

Water: Low to moderate

Soil: None

Temperature: Cool to warm

Angel wings

Caladium

Angel wings have some of the most beautiful, translucent and colourful leaves you will ever see, and make fabulous indoor statement plants during the warmer months. They die down over winter, and when the leaves start to wilt in autumn, you should begin to water them less. Lift the tubers from the soil after the leaves have completely dried, remove and discard the leaves, then store the tubers in a paper bag in a cool, dark cupboard until spring. Then plant them up and water sparingly until the shoots appear above the soil line. Angel wings love bright light and even direct morning sun will suit them perfectly.

Light: Direct morning to bright filtered

Water: Moderate

Soil: Jungle mix or core indoor mix

Temperature: Warm

Arrowhead plant

Syngonium

With many stunning hybrids to choose from, arrowhead plants are easy-care, vigorous growers that can trail, climb or sprawl outwards depending on how you decide to grow them. They can get leggy as they grow and will benefit from a good cut back in spring to keep them compact and attractive. Arrowhead plants tolerate a wide range of conditions; they prefer bright filtered light to stay compact but will grow in moderate light, too. Temperature wise, they like warmth but will go as low as 16°C without harm.

Light: Bright filtered to medium

Water: Moderate

Soil: Core indoor mix

Temperature: Cool to warm

Bird of paradise

Strelitzia nicolai

One of the best larger, architectural indoor plants, the giant bird of paradise is a pop classic when it comes to tropical foliage. They can be kept at a particular size for a number of years by repotting them into a pot of the same size. Sun lovers by nature, they perform best in direct to bright filtered light and will become elongated and less attractive if kept in low light for more than a few months at a time. They are tolerant of cooler conditions down to 12°C, but are at their best in the warm zone of 18–30°C.

Light: Direct morning to bright filtered

Water: Low to moderate

Soil: Core indoor mix

Temperature: Cool to warm

Bird's nest anthurium

Anthurium hookeri

The *Anthurium* genus is full of many spectacular plants and, of the group called 'bird's nest anthuriums', *hookeri* is one of the nicest, with wide, generous leaves sprouting from a central stem. They can grow to a couple of metres across outdoors in the tropics, but indoors they are more likely to reach about a metre in diameter. I love them because the classic shape of the leaves contrasts with the unusual growth habit to create a thoroughly interesting plant. Like most plants in this genus, they thrive in bright filtered light, but the bird's nest variety will also grow well in medium light, despite becoming less compact.

Light: Bright filtered to medium

Water: Moderate

Soil: Epiphyte and aroid mix

Temperature: Warm

Bird's nest fern

Asplenium nidus

This is one of the easier ferns to grow indoors, and I love to plant a few together in a pot for a super bushy look. The lime green of their glossy fronds is refreshing and pops against darker foliage. Like many ferns, they look their best when grown in bright filtered light, but will tolerate many light levels right through to low. My advice is to only leave them in low light for a couple of months at a time, rotating them with another shade-tolerant plant.

Light: Bright filtered to low

Water: Moderate

Soil: Core indoor mix

Temperature: Cool to warm

Black velvet alocasia

Alocasia reginula

Few plants channel tropical jungle vibes quite like the many species and varieties of alocasia: think spearhead-shaped leaves, contrasting veins and glorious green shades. The black velvet variety pictured here is particularly gorgeous with its dark, textural leaves. Alocasias are immensely popular at the moment but they can be challenging to care for because they have a tendency to go dormant. If the plant goes backwards and loses most or all of its leaves but the main stem remains firm and the roots healthy, water it just enough to keep the soil damp, keep it in a bright, warm position and wait for new growth to appear.

Light: Direct morning to bright filtered

Water: Moderate

Soil: Jungle mix

Temperature: Warm

Blushing bromeliad

Neoregelia carolinae 'Caroline Tricolor'

The Bromeliaceae or bromeliad family contains more than 3500 species of plants. Many of them originate from tropical South America and a lot are epiphytes: they grow on trees where their roots fasten them to branches while they collect water in an 'urn' created in the centre of the leaf structure. They are very adaptable and because of their small root volume and ability to survive variable conditions, bromeliads make ideal and exotic-looking indoor specimens. *Neoregelia* is a genus favoured by collectors, especially hybrids of *Neoregelia carolinae*, like the one pictured here, which turns from pink to red in the centre as it flowers. Keep the central cup or urn one-quarter full of water and no more or they tend to rot, especially in the colder months.

Light: Bright filtered to medium

Water: Moderate

Soil: Epiphyte and aroid mix

Temperature: Warm

Boston fern

Nephrolepis exaltata

When I think of the word 'fernery' I see images of white-painted rattan furniture, decorative glass windowpanes and huge Boston ferns hanging everywhere, such is the iconic nature of this plant. Actually, sometimes I wish I had a fern house just so I could grow them into the incredible specimens you see online. There are so many cultivars, each with a varying degree of laciness, that there's surely one to suit every home and collection. They need cool conditions with adequate moisture at the roots and bright filtered light to perform really well. Boston ferns will grow in medium light, too, but tend to be finer and more elongated over time, so if you want lush and bushy, brighter light is the key.

Light: Bright filtered to medium

Water: High

Soil: Core indoor mix

Temperature: Cool

Calico English ivy

Hedera helix 'Calico'

A beloved garden plant for centuries, English ivy is also grown indoors but it needs cooler temperatures to do well – so no dry, stuffy rooms for this specimen. It likes to dry out before it's rewatered, and also appreciates bright light and fresh air. Ivy looks amazing grown on wire shapes and supports, which can be found at your local nursery.

Light: Direct morning to bright filtered

Water: Low to moderate

Soil: Core indoor mix

Temperature: Cool

Caudiciform

Fockea edulis

Fockea is a caudiciform, a group of interesting plants very popular with collectors. They have swollen, water-storing root bases (caudices) that look a little like above-ground bulbs or trunks and usually sprout growth from the top of this, giving them a fascinating bonsai-like appearance. Caudiciforms even have their own collectors' clubs and Instagram pages! Most are pretty easy to grow provided you give them enough light and don't overwater during their dormant phase. When they're dormant you need to treat them like cacti and water very sparingly, just enough to stop the caudex from shrivelling. Increase watering once new shoots appear.

Light: Direct morning to bright filtered

Water: Moderate during the growing season, low in dormancy

Soil: Cacti and succulent mix

Temperature: Cool

Chestnut dioon

Dioon edule

The chestnut dioon is a cycad, a group of plants that have existed on earth for tens of millions of years. They are popular today for their striking palm-like leaves and hardiness. Chestnut dioons are one of the easiest cycads to grow, along with cardboard palms (*Zamia furfuracea*). They do best in bright filtered light, preferably with some morning sun, but are tolerant of medium to low light for a few months at a time. They are temperature hardy, too, and tolerant of large swings. Make sure you are careful of the leaf ends, which can be sharp.

Light: Direct morning to bright filtered

Water: Low to moderate

Soil: Core indoor mix

Temperature: Cool to warm

Chinese evergreen

Aglaonema 'Super White'

The Chinese evergreen is a staple for indoor plantscaping because it's one of the few plants that offers patterned and speckled leaves that will also tolerate low-light conditions and less than regular watering. 'Yay!' I hear you say – me too, because there are some great cultivars available now, such as this 'Super White', my favourite, which will glimmer in low-light situations and break up displays of all-green foliage beautifully. The greener varieties have the most stamina in lower light positions, with the red and pink toned leaves preferring brighter spots.

Light: Bright filtered to low

Water: Moderate

Soil: Core indoor mix

Temperature: Cool to warm

Chinese money plant

Pilea peperomioides

One of the pop stars of the plant world over the past few years, *Pilea peperomioides* has Instagram pages dedicated solely to pictures of it in cute pots, often lovingly held by an owner. At one stage folks were paying large amounts for tiny plants; now they're available almost anywhere at very reasonable prices. Keep removing the little 'pups' or plantlets if you want a feature plant with larger leaves, like this specimen, or leave them for a bushy look. They will lean towards the light, so turn them 180 degrees every couple of weeks to keep them evenly balanced.

Light: Bright filtered

Water: Moderate in summer, low in winter

Soil: Core indoor mix

Temperature: Cool

Coleus

Coleus scutellarioides 'Main Street Rodeo Drive'

Cool name, right?! Nothing beats the humble coleus for indoor foliage colour, in luminous shades of fuchsia, lime, yellow, purple, pastel pink, apricot, red ... there's even a dark blackish cultivar called 'Black Prince' and, of course, the gorgeous 'Main Street Rodeo Drive' pictured here. Coleus are best treated as annuals or biennials, meaning you'll want to throw them out after one or two seasons because they become untidy and unattractive. Two key tips: first, never let them develop flowers; if you do they'll go to seed and die, so pinch or snip off any flower buds. Second, start them from seedlings or cuttings in spring and regularly pinch out the growing shoots to encourage bushiness.

Light: Direct morning to bright filtered

Water: Moderate

Soil: Core indoor mix

Temperature: Cool to warm

Crystal anthurium

Anthurium crystallinum hybrid

Probably one of the hottest collectable indoor plants on the planet at the moment, the crystal anthurium is having its moment, although it's been the epitome of tropical beauty for many years. Social media has propelled it into the limelight because of its shimmering, velvet-textured leaves and silver contrasting veins and, although still not widely available, it is becoming more accessible and is often for sale online. It likes minimum temperatures of around 18°C and humidity of 50 per cent or higher, making it a good choice for a warm, well-lit bathroom. Put it in a beautiful planter and let it sparkle.

Light: Bright filtered to medium

Water: Moderate

Soil: Epiphyte and aroid mix

Temperature: Warm

Cyclamen

Cyclamen persicum

Cyclamen, such as the beautiful florist's cyclamen (*Cyclamen persicum*) pictured here, have been cultivated since the early seventeenth century and are one of the most beloved flowering indoor plants. The leaves are strikingly patterned, with the flowers held on dainty stems above the foliage. Cyclamen grow throughout autumn and winter and prefer cool, moist conditions – they definitely don't enjoy hot, dry rooms so if you don't have a cool area inside it's best to keep them on a porch, verandah or other undercover area outdoors. After flowering, the leaves will die back and the plant should be allowed to dry out until new signs of growth appear the following autumn, when watering can be gradually increased as growth speeds up.

Light: Bright filtered

Water: Moderate

Soil: Core indoor mix

Temperature: Cool

Dumb cane

Dieffenbachia 'Reflector'

The 'Reflector' cultivar is my favourite *Dieffenbachia*, with velvety leaves and an almost camo pattern in three different green tones. There are lots of hybrids available, though mostly in green and white variations, and they provide a welcome splash of pattern indoors, where they will grow happily for years provided they aren't kept soggy. Bright filtered light will keep them compact and in full colour (the leaves go darker and greener in low light). They can grow tall and leggy, but the tops of the plants can be cut off and treated as a cutting while the base will reshoot. Keep them away from pets and children as the sap can irritate the mouth and throat.

Light: Bright filtered to medium

Water: Moderate

Soil: Core indoor mix

Temperature: Warm

Elephant foot plant

Dioscorea elephantipes

This fascinating plant from Africa produces a very rough, cracked caudex (swollen base) as it grows, resembling an elephant's foot. The caudex can grow to a metre across but only after many years. Each season, as the weather cools down, it produces a vigorous vine covered in small, heart-shaped leaves that contrast perfectly with the rugged base. It loves bright light with some morning sun if possible, and needs almost no water when it is dormant. Temperature doesn't really worry this plant, and it can tolerate a wide range.

Light: Direct morning to bright filtered

Water: Moderate during the growing season, low in dormancy

Soil: Cacti and succulent mix

Temperature: Cool to warm

Fernleaf cactus

Selenicereus chrysocardium

The beautiful, large, leaf-like stems of this jungle cactus are flat and look wonderful tumbling out of pots and baskets – their verdant shade of green adds lushness to anywhere they're placed. The plant sometimes produces huge, white flowers with golden-yellow stamens, but these are more of a surprise than a regular occurrence. It's very easy to propagate this plant from stem sections about 15 cm in length popped into propagation mix (see page 248 for step-by-step instructions). The rooted sections can be potted back into the mother plant for a super spectacular, bushy specimen.

Light: Bright filtered

Water: Moderate

Soil: Epiphyte and aroid mix

Temperature: Cool to warm

Fiddle-leaf fig

Ficus lyrata

The fiddle-leaf fig takes its name from its attractive violin-shaped leaves. It is a striking indoor tree that can grow to a few metres tall inside if it's looked after well and not cut back. These figs are not the easiest plants to care for but their striking presence has led them to have loads of fans all over the world – and lucky for us they are far more readily available now than they were a few years ago. Fiddle-leaf figs like to dry out slightly between waterings and need to be situated in bright light to thrive. Some leaf-drop of the lower leaves is normal but too much or not enough water, cold temperatures and low light will cause more to drop – hence my nickname for this plant, 'the finnicky-leaf fig'.

Light: Direct morning to bright filtered

Water: Moderate

Soil: Core indoor mix

Temperature: Warm

Fishbone prayer plant

Ctenanthe burle-marxii

Another plant from the ever popular Marantaceae family, this prayer plant has a low growth habit that is a great foil for more upright plants and perfect for coffee and side tables where it won't get in the way of chatting or watching TV. This plant loves bright filtered light, but will grow very well in medium light, too. It's not so tolerant of cool temperatures, preferring no lower than 18°C.

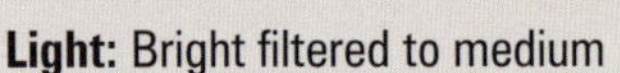

Light: Bright filtered to medium

Water: Moderate

Soil: Jungle mix

Temperature: Warm

Flamingo flower plant

Anthurium andraeanum

Lasting flowers are not common on indoor plants, but the flamingo flower plant produces exotic, glossy bracts in shades of red, white and pink that remain for weeks at a time. The flowers themselves are tiny and grow on a central spadix, which is a spike that protrudes from the shiny spathe. Even without its stunning blooms, the leaves themselves are a treat: heart shaped with a wonderful sheen on the end of delicately thin stems. This plant is native to tropical rainforests in Colombia and Ecuador, so that will give you a hint of the conditions they prefer. Warmth is a must, and it grows well in either an epiphyte mix or one slightly richer in organic matter.

Light: Bright filtered to medium

Water: Moderate

Soil: Epiphyte and aroid mix or jungle mix

Temperature: Warm

Grape ivy

Cissus rhombifolia 'Ellen Danica'

The grape ivy is a member of the grape family, which is how it gets its name. It's a terrific option for plant newbies as it will tolerate both relatively low-light areas and spasmodic watering. It's not fussy when it comes to soil, but will definitely benefit from a richer potting mix, such as my jungle mix, to be at its absolute best. I love this plant because it looks just as good climbing up a trellis as it does tumbling from a hanging basket or pot shelf.

Light: Bright filtered to low

Water: Moderate

Soil: Core indoor mix or jungle mix

Temperature: Cool to warm

Happy plant (variegated)

Dracaena fragrans 'Massangeana'

Happy plants have been a staple in commercial plantscapes and home interiors for decades. Their use goes even further back: in Europe these tropical African plants have appeared in homes since the mid 1800s, and they have been popular in the USA since the early 1900s. They are especially good at adding height to plant groupings in medium to lower light areas.

Light: Bright filtered to low

Water: Moderate

Soil: Core indoor mix

Temperature: Cool to warm

Hens and chicks

Echeveria elegans 'Grey Red'

Echeverias are the best succulents, with many cool varieties offering different colours, shapes and sizes. The 'Grey Red' cultivar pictured here is a smaller one that has a wonderful blue–green colour and compact, clumping rosettes, making it perfect for indoors. *Echeverias* need bright light with some direct light to stay compact and in full colour, so if you can't give them that inside, try rotating them between a sunny balcony and indoors for a month at a time.

Light: Direct morning

Water: Moderate during the growing season, low in winter

Soil: Cacti and succulent mix or core indoor mix

Temperature: Cool to warm

Iron cross begonia

Begonia masoniana

The iron cross begonia has been in cultivation since the 1950s and it's easy to see why. The large, handsome leaves combine deep, rich green and a burgundy-to-brown central cross with a puckered texture that adds to the drama. They're easier to grow than rex begonias and the perfect foil to plants with plain leaves in groupings. Turn the plant every couple of weeks to keep its symmetry. The iron cross begonia hails from China and Vietnam, and it prefers cooler nights (around 16°C), but will tolerate temperatures as low as 14°C for limited periods. Daytime temperatures around 22–26°C are perfect.

Light: Bright filtered

Water: Moderate

Soil: Jungle mix

Temperature: Cool

Kentia palm

Howea forsteriana

Did you know that the world's most popular indoor palm is an Australian native? Endemic to Lord Howe Island off the coast of New South Wales, the kentia palm has been popular since the Victorian era because it thrives in buildings where cool temperatures and low light and humidity are too challenging for other palm species. These robust qualities make the kentia by far the best choice for an indoor palm, as well as the fact that it is relatively slow growing – buy one that is nearly the size you want and it will remain a good size for a few years. They are more expensive than faster growing palms, but in my opinion their graceful beauty is worth it.

Light: Bright filtered to low

Water: Moderate

Soil: Core indoor mix

Temperature: Cool to warm

Madagascar palm

Pachypodium lamerei

Madagascar palms are striking plants that can grow up to 2 metres tall indoors over a long period of time. The long trunk is covered with thick spines and leaves sprout from the top of the trunk, giving it a very modern, sculptural appearance. This plant needs sun and the more light you can give it indoors the better – though be careful, as always, to avoid scorching if you have direct sun shining through glass onto its leaves. I love to display the Madagascar palm with other tropical plants that complement its exotic appearance.

Light: Direct morning to bright filtered

Water: Low

Soil: Cacti and succulent mix

Temperature: Warm

Maidenhair fern

Adiantum raddianum 'Pacific Maid'

Surely this is one of the prettiest ferns there ever was? I especially love the dense, compact cultivar pictured here, 'Pacific Maid'. The perennial maidenhair fern is beloved and bemoaned at the same time. Those who can grow it well are viewed as wizards, while others find it an impossible beauty, a fern to be admired when freshly bought and discarded when it eventually dies. Well, the good news is that providing a few key things will virtually guarantee you success. Give it bright, filtered light (absolutely no direct sun) and constant moisture during the warmer months; sit it in a shallow tray of water and let it dry out for no more than a day or two. Also key is to avoid dry, overheated conditions, which will dehydrate the delicate fronds. Stick to these tips and you'll have no problems with the maidenhair fern.

Light: Bright filtered

Water: High

Soil: Jungle mix

Temperature: Cool

Mistletoe cactus

Rhipsalis campos-portoanum

Rhipsalis are jungle cacti that grow in rainforests, so unlike desert cacti they will grow in lower light but they need more water than their desert cousins. They are some of the best trailing plants for indoor displays, with so many amazing stem forms that lend a sculptural element to vertical space. *Rhipsalis campos-portoanum*, pictured here, is one of the finer, prettier jungle cacti, but when it fills out it is stunning and it will eventually grow to a couple of metres long, though you can prune it back if it gets too unruly. Because they can grow in a wide variety of conditions – bright to medium light and cool to warm temperatures – *Rhipsalis* are some of the best indoor plants to grow. Their succulent form and ability to withstand dryness also makes them fabulous for beginners.

Light: Bright filtered to medium

Water: Moderate during the growing season, low in winter

Soil: Core indoor mix

Temperature: Cool to warm

Moth orchid

Phalaenopsis

Instant elegance is how I summarise the effect of the moth orchid on an interior. I have been in love with them since I was a child, when they were very hard to come by, and over the years it's been joyous watching them become freely available, appearing in supermarkets and hardware stores alike. I don't know of an indoor plant with longer lasting blooms – I have had some last for 6 months or more – and find keeping them on the drier side helps the blooms last longer. Once the flowers do die, cut the flower stem off to the third or fourth node or notch on the stem. Keep looking after it, and often it will produce a new flower spike from the old one. Despite what you read elsewhere, don't use ice cubes to water your moth orchid, as they do more damage than good. Just pour half a cup of water onto dry moss if they are planted in that, or give them a good water if they are in orchid bark.

Light: Bright filtered to medium

Water: Low to moderate

Soil: Epiphyte and aroid mix

Temperature: Warm

Old man cactus

Left: *Cephalocereus senilis*
Right: *Oreocereus trollii*

I'm a great fan of indoor cacti. They have such a wonderful, arid, sculptural vibe that evokes scenes of sun-drenched deserts and exotic locales. It may seem obvious to say but desert plants like a lot of light. They enjoy direct sun – however, I grow these old man cacti beside a north-facing window that has frosted glass, where they only ever get bright filtered light, and they also thrive there. Water them sparingly – once every 4–6 weeks in winter and once a fortnight in summer – and keep water off the plants themselves. Oh, and a pastry brush or old toothbrush works wonders to fluff out the hairs and remove any dust that accumulates.

Light: Direct morning to bright filtered

Water: Low

Soil: Cacti and succulent mix

Temperature: Cool to warm

Ox tongue plant

Gasteria carinata var. *verrucosa*

Native to South Africa, these succulents have leaves arranged symmetrically opposite each other, giving a very modern appearance. Some varieties, such as *verrucosa* pictured here, have wonderful texture, while others have stripes along their leaves. They are easy to care for provided you can give them the bright light they need to stay compact and thrive.

Light: Direct morning to bright filtered

Water: Low

Soil: Cacti and succulent mix

Temperature: Cool

Peace lily (variegated)

Spathiphyllum wallisii 'Picasso'

The peace lily is another A-list house plant with so many good qualities it's a no-brainer that you should have at least one in your home. Of course, you'll find the plain green variety in every nursery and plant shop; 'Picasso', the lovely cultivar pictured here, is not as widely available but well worth searching out if you love variegated plants. Why are peace lilies such great plants? Well, they will take all manner of abuse and barely raise an eyebrow (or leaf!), maintaining their glossy green foliage and rewarding their owner with pure white flowers that appear throughout spring and last for a couple of months. If they wilt for a day or two, water them well and they will perk back up again. They will tolerate low light and drier air as well.

Light: Bright filtered to low

Water: High in summer, moderate in winter

Soil: Core indoor mix

Temperature: Cool to warm

Ponytail palm

Beaucarnea recurvata

The long, narrow leaves of the ponytail palm are like a green firework exploding from the top of its bottle-shaped trunk. The ponytail palm is actually not a palm at all; in fact, it's related to asparagus. It's very drought tolerant and can go weeks or even months with no water. I think the ponytail palm is undervalued as a house plant, because there aren't many plants as sculptural as this, especially as it matures.

Light: Direct morning to bright filtered

Water: Low

Soil: Core indoor mix or cacti and succulent mix

Temperature: Cool to warm

Pothos (variegated)

Epipremnum aureum 'Marble Queen'

Also known by numerous other names, including devil's ivy, pothos is one of the most widely grown and loved indoor plants, and it is perfect for beginners and experts alike. I do love some of the more unusual varieties, like the variegated one pictured here, but even the plain greens plants make a lovely addition to any interior. All varieties will grow much larger leaves if trained on a totem – some will grow leaves up to a metre long when they climb trees in the wild. They make great trailers, too, and grow easily from stem and tip cuttings (see page 248 for step-by-step instructions on how to do this). Because of their ability to grow in almost any situation, I keep a few smaller plants that I have grown from cuttings as little accent plants that I pop into groupings all over my house. Moderate watering will keep pothos looking their best – if they are allowed to dry out for too long, they will drop some lower leaves.

Light: Direct morning to low

Water: Moderate

Soil: Core indoor mix or epiphyte and aroid mix

Temperature: Cool to warm

Prayer plant (variegated)

Goeppertia 'White Fusion'

Goeppertia come in many different varieties, but this variegated beauty combines different shades of green with pure white patches on the front of its leaves, with pink to purple hues on the back. Add to this wavy, ruffled leaf edges and you have one of the most desired indoor plants of the past few years. I've nicknamed it 'white confusion' because it can be difficult to master but here are my tips: it likes a shallow pot with rich, free-draining soil and you need to let it dry only slightly before watering well. Spider mites love this plant, so I spray mine with rose spray every 4 weeks in the growing season. Generally prayer plants like warm conditions with humidity over 50 per cent and bright filtered light to be at their best. They are famous for getting dry leaf edges, which you can simply trim off, along with any leaves that have turned yellow with age.

Light: Bright filtered to medium

Water: Moderate

Soil: Jungle mix

Temperature: Warm

Purple shamrock

Oxalis triangularis

A shamrock-shaped leaf at the end of each fine long stem gives this plant the appearance of a flock of richly coloured butterflies hovering over a pot. I love it for its unique colouration – pops of deep purple and pink among the many shades of green – and ease of care. It will go dormant if it gets too warm, so this plant is one for a cooler part of the house. If it does go dormant, I suggest watering very occasionally and only enough to slightly moisten the soil; wait until new shoots appear, then start to increase watering again.

Light: Bright filtered

Water: Moderate

Soil: Core indoor mix

Temperature: Cool

Red stripe prayer plant

Maranta leuconeura var. *erythroneura*

Prayer plants are from the family Marantaceae and are so named because the leaves fold up in pairs at dusk to resemble hands folded in prayer. They are something of a classic because of their stunning leaves that are often iridescent and gorgeously coloured, like this red stripe one, which comes from the Brazilian rainforest where it grows on the forest floor. Because this plant creeps naturally, it can become leggy quite quickly. My fix for this is to cut the elongated stems off with at least one node, root them in water or propagation mix (see page 248 for step-by-step instructions) and plant them back into the centre of the mother plant by digging a little hole with the end of a spoon.

Light: Bright filtered to medium

Water: Moderate

Soil: Jungle mix

Temperature: Warm

Rex begonia

Begonia 'Lightning Strike'

With hundreds of cultivars bearing jewel-like colours on textured, iridescent leaves, rex begonias are a sight to behold. However, they are fussy blighters and especially delicate when it comes to watering. While classed as liking moderate water, it's best to keep them on the dryer side, allowing the soil to almost dry completely before watering again, but preferably before or just after they begin to wilt. Keep water off the leaves, if you can, as dampness encourages fungal disease.

Light: Bright filtered to medium

Water: Moderate

Soil: Jungle mix

Temperature: Cool to warm

Rik-rak cactus

Disocactus anguliger

Also known as the zig zag or fishbone cactus, this exotic-looking forest cactus is an epiphyte that grows in trees in its native Mexico. Its fishbone-like stems climb upwards, attaching themselves to the tree with aerial roots as they go. It's most often grown as a trailer indoors, where it lends a distinctive appearance to shelves and hanging baskets. I love to send its stems tumbling over the edges of tables. *Disocactus* enjoy some direct morning light if they can get it and are not fussy regarding their soil as long as it is free draining. I have found that my core mix is fine, but they tend to do a bit better with jungle mix, as it most closely resembles the conditions their roots encounter in their natural environment.

Light: Direct morning to bright filtered

Water: Moderate in summer, low in winter

Soil: Jungle mix or core indoor mix

Temperature: Cool to warm

Rubber plant (variegated)

Ficus elastica 'Tineke'

The humble rubber plant has come a long way, with beautiful cultivars, such as 'Tineke' pictured here, now gracing our homes. Its large and classic-shaped leaves are thick and waxy, and the plant will grow into a small tree indoors. It is much easier to look after than its cousin, the fiddle-leaf fig, as it is far more drought and temperature tolerant. *Ficus elastica* will tolerate dryness for a couple of weeks at a time, but it won't do well if over watered and will drop lower leaves if allowed to stay wet. It will be fine as low as 10°C if kept dryer. Look out for the other cultivars, such as 'Burgundy', which has deep maroon, almost black, leaves and 'Ruby', flushed with a beautiful pink.

Light: Bright filtered to medium

Water: Moderate in summer, low in winter

Soil: Core indoor mix

Temperature: Warm

Satin pothos

Scindapsus pictus 'Exotica'

Satin pothos is a member of the Araceae family that has become a common indoor plant around the world, and this 'Exotica' cultivar is one of my personal favourites because of its large, silvery leaves. I prefer to grow it on a totem because it produces bigger leaves, but it looks great as a trailing plant, too. Satin pothos will grow in medium light quite well, but likes warmth and doesn't tolerate temperatures below 16°C for long.

Light: Bright filtered to medium

Water: Moderate in summer, low in winter

Soil: Core indoor mix or epiphyte and aroid mix

Temperature: Warm

Shingle plant

Rhaphidophora cryptantha

Shingle plants display a very particular growth habit: they tightly hug the surface they grow against. And while they will grow without a support, they will be spindly, with small leaves. Give them a totem or flat piece of wood or bark to grow on and they'll come into their own, with their wonderful leaves displayed at their very best.

Light: Bright filtered to medium

Water: Moderate

Soil: Epiphyte and aroid mix or sphagnum moss

Temperature: Warm

Silver snake plant

Dracaena trifasciata 'Moonshine'

The snake plant is my favourite plant for beginners and serial plant killers because it is so hardy. It will put up with low light and low water, as well as no repotting for years and cold to warm conditions. It comes in a range of varieties, including the elegant, silvery 'Moonshine' pictured here. Its vertical growth habit and leaf patterns are very retro and reminiscent of mid-century interiors, in which it was used extensively. It's been popular ever since. You may know snake plants as *Sansevierias*, but they have been reclassified as *Dracaena*.

Light: Direct morning to low

Water: Moderate to low

Soil: Core indoor mix

Temperature: Cool to warm

Spider plant (variegated)

Chlorophytum comosum 'Variegatum'

I understand if you really don't like the spider plant because it reminds you of your Aunty Beryl's house (sorry Aunty Beryl!). It does have a reputation as an unattractively common indoor plant, but I encourage you to revisit this wonderful specimen if you haven't already. I used to be a naysayer, but once I saw it hanging from the ceiling of my home and watched it thrive with very little care, it totally won me over!

Light: Direct morning to low

Water: Moderate

Soil: Core indoor mix

Temperature: Cool to warm

Spiderwort (variegated)

Tradescantia fluminensis 'Variegata'

Spiderworts, or inch plants, are a staple of the indoor jungle and very easy to care for. The white stripy variety pictured here happens to be a favourite of mine, and as long as it gets bright light it seems to be happy. Spiderwort can become long and straggly after a while, at which point a good trim in spring quickly results in new growth and a refreshed plant. I root the cuttings (see page 248 for step-by-step instructions on how to do this) and then plant them back into the pot for fullness. Look out for the tricolor and purple varieties, too!

Light: Bright filtered

Water: Moderate

Soil: Core indoor mix

Temperature: Cool to warm

String of hearts

Ceropegia woodii

Also known as chain of hearts, this is a gorgeous, romantic succulent that adds delicacy to any indoor display with its pillowy, heart-shaped leaves and long, fine trailing stems. If left to do its thing, it will trail many metres, but you can also wind the stems around and around the top of the pot for a bushier effect. String of hearts grows from small bulbs which will rot if overwatered, so be on the cautious side rather than generous with water.

Light: Direct morning to bright filtered

Water: Low

Soil: Cacti and succulent mix

Temperature: Cool

String of pearls

Senecio rowleyanus

The unique form of string of pearls makes it a highlight in any collection, and it's particularly striking when it's allowed to tumble onto tabletops or out of a hanging basket. Make sure you keep the plant close to the top of the pot as it requires good air circulation and anything that prevents this, even a centimetre or so of pot above the top of the soil, will make it vulnerable to rot. It also needs lots of light to stay compact and healthy. Look out for the beautiful variegated variety with cream stripes.

Light: Direct morning to bright filtered

Water: Low

Soil: Cacti and succulent mix

Temperature: Cool

Swiss cheese plant (variegated)

Monstera deliciosa 'Thai Constellation'

When I'm asked which is my favourite indoor plant I always say Swiss cheese plant in all its varieties! Of these, there are some with more delicacy and others with more enticing colour, such as the 'Thai Constellation' pictured here. Variegated varieties are beautiful but more expensive and not as widely available; if you can't find one, the plain green version still ticks all the boxes. Easy to find: tick; affordable: tick; tolerant of varying light, water, soil and temperature: tick. Add to this its incredible, iconic look and this is why I call it the little black dress of house plants.

Light: Direct morning to medium

Water: Moderate

Soil: Core indoor mix or epiphyte and aroid mix

Temperature: Cool to warm

Tiger bromeliad

Vriesea 'Tiger Tim'

Vriesea is another genus of the Bromeliad family that loves indoor cultivation, and this striped cultivar, 'Tiger Tim', is a standout beauty. Like most 'broms', they do well in a smallish pot for the size of the plant, preferring snug roots rather than lots of empty mix. Contrary to popular belief, it is not essential to keep the central urn of a bromeliad filled with water – in fact, this is a sure way to rot the plant. These plants are particularly sensitive to overfilling the cup, so let them dry for 2–7 days at a time depending on the temperature, and, if it's cool, only a tiny bit of water is needed. In winter, leave the urn dry and water the roots every 2–3 weeks or so instead, when the soil has dried out.

Light: Bright filtered to medium

Water: Moderate

Soil: Epiphyte and aroid mix

Temperature: Warm

Toothed philodendron

Philodendron lacerum

The variety of leaf shapes in the *Philodendron* genus is mind boggling, from huge, heart-shaped leaves to fern-like fronds and everything in between – this is why they are so desirable to us plant nuts. The toothed 'philo' pictured here displays a lobed leaf that looks fabulous when mixed with other leaf shapes or when the plant is used as a feature specimen on its own. Like other philodendrons, it can grow large and needs to have the top cut off when it gets too tall. You can use the top as a tip cutting to make another plant, leaving the base to reshoot (see page 260 for step-by-step instructions on how to do this).

Light: Bright filtered to medium

Water: Moderate

Soil: Epiphyte and aroid mix

Temperature: Warm

Umbrella plant (dwarf)

Schefflera arboricola

Both the full-size umbrella plant and this dwarf version add a lushness and texture to your indoor plant world. They are very easy to care for and can be allowed to grow upright and tall or trimmed to encourage a fuller specimen. There are some cool variegated varieties, too, and they will tolerate a wide range of light conditions, from direct morning all the way through to low.

Light: Direct morning to low

Water: Moderate

Soil: Core indoor mix

Temperature: Warm

Vanda orchid

Vanda

One of the elements I love about orchids is the often incongruous combination of their leaves and flowers. Vandas are a perfect example: they have a regimented and rather controlled arrangement of strappy leaves mixed with an explosion of colour and texture in their stunning flowers. They make perfect statement plants on a coffee table and once the flowers are finished the plant, with its exposed aerial roots, makes a fascinating addition to groupings.

Light: Direct morning to bright filtered

Water: Moderate

Soil: Epiphyte and aroid mix

Temperature: Warm

Velvet philodendron

Philodendron hederaceum

The *Philodendron* genus includes a large number of plants, many of which are grown indoors for their beautiful leaves and striking forms. A number have velvety leaves, and the velvet philodendron pictured here – one of the 'it' plants of the moment – is the easiest of these to obtain and care for. It's a climbing plant in the wild, where it will eventually develop 30 cm leaves that lose their velvety patina at maturity – but there's no need to worry! It's highly unlikely to reach that size inside. It can be grown as a trailer or on a totem, where it will develop larger, deep emerald leaves up to 20 cm long. Either way, it's a gorgeous plant and a worthy addition to your home.

Light: Bright filtered to medium

Water: Moderate

Soil: Epiphyte and aroid mix

Temperature: Cool to warm

Watermelon peperomia

Peperomia argyreia

Definitely the favourite in this popular genus, the watermelon peperomia has adorable, striped, succulent leaves in perfect tones of silver and blue green. It will grow towards the light so turn it 180 degrees every couple of weeks. It's also very fragile, so handle with care when moving it as its leaves tend to drop off easily. Overwatering is the main cause of failure with the watermelon 'pep'. It likes to be on the dry side before it is watered again, and try to keep water off the leaves and stems, especially in cold weather.

Light: Bright filtered

Water: Moderate to low

Soil: Core indoor mix

Temperature: Cool to warm

Wax plant (variegated)

Hoya 'Krimson Queen'

Let me wax lyrical about wax plants … these wonderful trailing or climbing plants make perfect indoor companions. There are many cultivars and species to choose from, such as the 'Krimson Queen' pictured here, and numerous clubs and societies dedicated to collecting and growing them. Maybe it's the beautiful, waxy leaves that come in so many different sizes, colours and patterns, or perhaps it's the unique, often highly fragrant, velvet flowers held in clusters on the ends of short stems that make them so popular? Whatever the case, the *Hoya* genus has something for everyone.

Light: Bright filtered to medium

Water: Moderate

Soil: Jungle mix

Temperature: Cool to warm

Zebra plant

Haworthiopsis fasciata

This little cutie is the perfect size for small decorative containers. I use the zebra plant in lots of groupings where its clearly defined, zebra-like stripes add a pop of pattern and interest. This hardy succulent tolerates low light for a couple of months at a time; just keep it dry. It's so fuss free every plant collector needs at least one to brighten up a windowsill or side table. A bonus of the zebra plant is that it readily produces offsets that are very easy to pull from the main plant and propagate – the perfect gift for your plant-loving pals.

Light: Direct morning to bright filtered

Water: Low

Soil: Cacti and succulent mix or core indoor mix

Temperature: Cool to warm

Zebra prayer plant

Goeppertia zebrina

One of the most beautiful of the prayer plants, the zebra has velvety leaves with glistening stripes of emerald and lime. Like many in the Marantaceae family, its underground rhizomes send up new shoots of leaves as they spread. The older leaves will start to die back as they are replaced with the new, so regularly trim off the tired foliage to keep the plant looking fresh.

Light: Bright filtered to medium

Water: Moderate

Soil: Jungle mix

Temperature: Warm

ZZ plant

Zamioculcas zamiifolia 'Jungle Warrior'

One of the toughest indoor plants there is, I recommend the ZZ plant to newbies, people who are serial plant killers and those who simply want zero fuss. ZZ plants store water in their swollen stems and roots and are not only tolerant of underwatering but also of a wide range of light conditions: they're one of the few plants that will survive in very low light for extended periods of time. There are a few different varieties available now, including a dwarf variety and the 'Jungle Warrior' pictured here, which has very dark, almost black leaves and bright green new growth.

Light: Bright filtered to low

Water: Low

Soil: Core indoor mix

Temperature: Cool to warm

SOIL, POTS & REPOTTING

Potting mix 101

Finding your soil-mate

All excellent gardeners know that good gardening starts with the basics. One of the most important is soil or, in the case of indoor plants, potting mix. Indoor potting mix shouldn't be the same as soil from the garden, and there's a reason for this – roots in the ground are not contained within the walls of a pot, but our indoor specimens will live their whole lives in a pot, and they need a mix that will help them deal with the challenges of a smaller space. For best results, it's essential to match the right potting mix with the right plant. Indoor plants originate from natural environments that vary greatly, ranging from lush and fecund rainforests to arid deserts. The roots of each type of plant have evolved to function optimally when growing in the kinds of soil they would encounter in their original environment.

As well as providing a substrate for roots to fasten onto and secure the plant, potting mix needs to provide nutrients and water, and allow for drainage and aeration. Not everyone knows this, but plant roots need air to survive! If a potting mix doesn't drain well, it gets waterlogged, which means that water replaces the air. In an airless environment fungi and bacteria multiply and the plant's roots rot and die. To keep a plant's root system in tiptop shape, there must be gaps in the substrate for the air to get in. Healthy roots are essential for growing strong plant specimens that thrive and grow larger with time, as they would in nature. One of the first things I consider when faced with a sick plant is its roots – how they look and feel. Firm, healthy roots with plenty of new root tips are the goal, while dark, soft or mushy roots are a sign of a problem. A plant's roots are a key indicator of how a specimen is doing, and that's why it's vitally important to start with the right potting mix.

Making your own potting mix

If you've ever Googled potting mix recipes, you'll have found that there are lots of them. Some are quite complicated, with numerous ingredients that may not all be easy to come by. The thought of having to traipse around the nursery to buy tons of product and then measure it out makes me feel exhausted, and that's before I've even left the house. We've all got enough to worry about! Many of us have got limited space and, let's face it, it's a hassle to mix all the components from ten different bags.

It really doesn't need to be that difficult – unless, of course, you are a diehard plant fanatic who loves spending hours slaving over a hot wheelbarrow full of rotted leaf litter and coarse scoria. If you are, I celebrate your dedication. However, if you want to keep things simple, I've spent the past few decades experimenting with different combinations and below are six easy mixes that will have your plants jumping out of their pots with joy. You will find lists of plants suitable for each of the mixes below in the following pages. I've listed each plant under the potting mix that it will grow *best* in, though some plants can be grown in more than one type of soil. There are some easy-growing plants, for example, that will do fine in my core indoor mix, but to grow a star specimen, you'll need one of the other more specialised potting mixes, such as jungle or epiphyte and aroid mix. For the full range of soil each plant can be grown in, see the A–Z of indoor plants on page 15.

- **Core indoor mix (see page 84)**
- **Epiphyte and aroid mix (see page 88)**
- **Cacti and succulent mix (see page 90)**
- **Jungle mix (see page 92)**
- **Propagation mix (see page 94)**
- **Light mix (see page 95)**

Getting prepared

I recommend buying a small trowel as well as a portable plastic potting tray to mix your soil in. If you're lucky enough to have an outdoor area, such as a balcony, courtyard or garden, you can prepare your mixes in these areas, but there are indoor options, too. The laundry, garage and even kitchen are all great places – my kitchen bench is my favourite work surface. If you want to make up a larger amount of mix, a plastic kitchen tidy or storage bin doubles as an excellent potting mix holder. Wear gardening gloves to keep your hands clean, if you prefer, and always remember to work in a well-ventilated area and follow the instructions on the bag when handling soil and soil additives. All of the ingredients in the following potting mixes are available at most nurseries and hardware stores.

Essential ingredients for your potting mixes

Any good chef knows the key to a delicious dish is quality ingredients, and the same is true for creating the soil your indoor plants live in. These essential ingredients and ready-made mixes will enable you to create a range of potting mixes that support healthy root systems and result in glowing, vital plants. All of the items below are readily available from nurseries, garden centres and hardware stores in a range of sizes to suit your needs.

Premium potting mix

Any premium potting mix is fine. I find that premium varieties work much better than the more basic options.

Cacti and succulent mix

This ready-made mix contains lots of gravel and sand, and is perfect for plants that like to grow in fast-draining and fast-drying soils.

Horticultural charcoal

Charcoal is often a part of the soil in forest environments. It absorbs impurities and provides texture and openness.

Perlite

Perlite is expanded volcanic glass. It is light, adds air pockets and holds moisture, which encourages healthy root systems.

Peat moss or coir peat

Peat moss and coir peat (also called coco peat) both retain moisture and add organic matter to the mix, which is ideal for jungle plants, which like a richer soil.

Orchid potting mix

This ready-made mix contains bark chips in different sizes. It's perfect for epiphytes and aroids as it is similar to the soil found in forests.

CORE INDOOR MIX

I use this potting mix for most of the plants I grow – snake plants, ficus, peace lilies and caladiums, to name a few.

The magic bullet for creating a good basic potting mix is perlite, a product made from expanded volcanic glass. I put it in everything – in the same way that chefs use salt and pepper, I use perlite. While not suitable as a growing medium on its own, perlite is ideal for adding into pre-made potting mixes to supercharge their performance. It keeps a mix friable, moderates moisture and, most importantly, creates spaces for air.

The potting mix that your plants are growing in starts to break down and compact over time. The soil in indoor pots is especially prone to this because drainage is usually not as good as in pots that are outdoors, and the extra moisture encourages the growth of microorganisms that break down its organic materials. Perlite is inorganic and so, as other parts of the mix start to crumble, it retains its shape and acts as a kind of scaffold that holds the soil open for longer. Its porous surface means water clings to it, while its expanded internal structure means air can easily penetrate it. In this way, it provides oxygen and water, and therefore helps to create the perfect environment for roots to flourish.

YOU WILL NEED:

- 5 parts premium potting mix
- 1 part perlite

I know this indoor mix will sound too simple to be effective, but I challenge you to give it a try. In a large tub, mix the potting mix and perlite well so that the perlite is evenly distributed throughout. That's it! I usually make this mix on the day I want to use it as it's so easy to put together, but you can prepare a big batch in advance if you like. I have had so much feedback over the years on how effective it is to simply add perlite, and the results speak for themselves!

TIP:

I always buy premium potting mix for my indoor plants. It's only a few dollars extra and if you buy the cheap stuff you won't get as good results. A potting mix that conforms to the Australian standard for premium potting mix will have a red box with a row of five ticks on the front of the bag.

Use core indoor mix for:

- Arrowhead plant (*Syngonium*)
- Bird of paradise (*Strelitzia*)
- Bird's nest fern (*Asplenium nidus*)
- Cane-stemmed begonias (such as *Begonia acutifolia*, *Begonia coccinea*, *Begonia maculata*)
- Chinese evergreen (*Aglaonema*)
- Chinese money plant (*Pilea peperomioides*)
- Coleus
- Cordylines
- Cycads, including Chestnut dioon (*Dioon edule*)
- Cyclamen
- Dumb cane (*Dieffenbachia*)
- English ivy (*Hedera helix*)
- Ferns, including Boston fern (*Nephrolepis exaltata*)
- Ficus, including the fiddle-leaf fig (*Ficus lyrata*), weeping fig (*Ficus benjamina*) and rubber plant (*Ficus elastica*)
- Happy plant (*Dracaena fragrans*)
- Mistletoe cacti (*Rhipsalis campos-portoanum*)
- Palms (most varieties)
- Peace lily (*Spathiphyllum*)
- Purple shamrock (*Oxalis triangularis*)
- Snake plant (*Dracaena*)
- Spider plant (*Chlorophytum comosum*)
- Spiderwort (*Tradescantia*)
- Umbrella plant (*Schefflera*)
- Watermelon peperomia (*Peperomia argyreia*)
- ZZ plant (*Zamioculcas zamiifolia*)

‘The magic bullet for creating a good basic potting mix is perlite, a product made from expanded volcanic glass. I put it in everything – in the same way that chefs use salt and pepper, I use perlite.’

EPIPHYTE & AROID MIX

A true epiphyte is a plant that grows in a tree or on a rock, usually in a jungle or forest setting. Epiphytes comprise some of the most popular and well-known indoor plants including bromeliads and orchids, as well as epiphytic aroids, such as pothos (*Epipremnum*), Swiss cheese plants (*Monstera deliciosa*) and philodendrons. Not all of the plants suited to this mix are epiphytes, because some may spend all or part of their lives growing on a mat of leaf litter on a forest floor – however, they all need larger particles in their potting mix as a result of where they come from. Epiphytic aroids are members of the plant family Araceae, and they're some of the most stunning plants in my collection. I credit this particular potting mix as part of the reason why I have so much success with them.

The orchid potting mix used here is a general purpose one – sometimes called cymbidium mix – made primarily from bark in different sizes, or grades. The bark chunks in the orchid mix replicate the environment of a forest, and the roots of these plants love to grab hold of them. The horticultural charcoal absorbs impurities and adds texture, while the perlite keeps it open and aerated.

YOU WILL NEED:

- 5 parts orchid potting mix
- 1 part horticultural charcoal
- 1 part perlite

In a large tub, mix the orchid potting mix, horticultural charcoal and perlite together well, making sure the charcoal and perlite are evenly distributed throughout the potting mix.

Use epiphyte and aroid mix for:

- Anthuriums, including bird's nest anthurium (*Anthurium hookeri*)
- Bromeliads (such as *Aechmea*, *Guzmania*, *Neoregelia*, *Vriesea*)
- Fernleaf cacti (*Selenicereus chrysocardium*)
- Orchids, including the moth orchid (*Phalaenopsis*) and vanda orchid
- Philodendrons
- Pothos (*Epipremnum*)
- Rhaphidophoras
- Satin pothos (*Scindapsus pictus*)
- Swiss cheese plant (*Monstera deliciosa*)

CACTI & SUCCULENT MIX

This mix is for all those plants that come from arid conditions. I use it for plants that like to dry out really quickly, such as cacti and most succulents. It has extra sand or grit to make it fast draining so it won't hold excess moisture. Instead of mixing my own, I simply buy a pre-made mix from my local nursery because I've found any quality mix works perfectly well without adjustment.

A quick note on jungle cacti, which are so popular at the moment. Although pre-made cacti and succulent mix is suitable for most plants in this category, I don't use it for jungle cacti because they don't come from arid environments. Instead I use my jungle mix (see page 92), which retains water and has more of the nutrients that they love.

Use cacti and succulent mix for:

- Arid-growing succulents, including *Agave*, *Aloe*, *Gasteria*, *Haworthia*
- Caudiciforms (most varieties, including *Fockea edulis*)
- Desert cacti
- Elephant foot plant (*Dioscorea elephantipes*)
- Hens and chicks (*Echeveria*)
- Madagascar palm (*Pachypodium lamerei*)
- Ponytail palm (*Beaucarnea recurvata*)
- String of hearts (*Ceropegia woodii*)
- String of pearls (*Senecio rowleyanus*)

JUNGLE MIX

I use this potting mix for tropical plants that need a bit more organic matter and moisture than the epiphytes. These tend to be plants that grow in moist forest environments in a substrate that is rich in decaying matter but still free draining. The floor of a jungle is actually a shallow layer of organic matter made up of things like decomposing leaves, branches and charcoal from old fires.

The peat moss or coir peat that we add to this mix can hold up to twenty times its weight in water. The combination of moss or peat with perlite and charcoal, which work to keep the mix open, provides the perfect medium to grow jungle plants. Charcoal is naturally anti-microbial and, because of its structure, it is also very porous and can absorb impurities. As well as helping protect the roots from harmful fungi and bacteria, it adds pockets of air to the soil.

YOU WILL NEED:

- 5 parts premium potting mix
- 1 part perlite
- 1 part peat moss or coir peat
- 1 part horticultural charcoal

In a large tub, mix the potting mix, perlite, peat moss or coir peat and charcoal together well – an even distribution will make sure your plants get the most from each ingredient.

Use jungle mix for:

- African violet (*Saintpaulia ionantha*)
- Alocasias
- Begonias (including iron cross, rex and rhizomatous)
- Caladiums
- Flamingo flower plant (*Anthurium andraeanum*)
- Gloxinia (*Sinningia speciosa*)
- Grapy ivy (*Cissus rhombifolia*)
- Jungle cacti (*Rhipsalis*, *Epiphyllum*)
- Maidenhair fern (*Adiantum*)
- Prayer plants (*Ctenanthe*, *Goeppertia*, *Maranta*, *Stromanthe*)
- Rik-rak cacti (*Disocactus anguliger*)
- Wax plant (*Hoya*)

PROPAGATION MIX

The best medium to grow offsets, runners and stem and leaf cuttings is a mix that is low in organic matter and free draining, but that will be able to retain moisture. Moisture is important to encourage new roots to form and prevent the cuttings from drying out, but the mix also needs to be open enough to allow small, delicate roots to grow through it and air to penetrate it. The presence of air discourages rot and fungal infections from developing and increases the likelihood of successful rooting.

YOU WILL NEED:

- 1 part propagating sand or perlite
- 1 part coir peat

Combine the propagating sand or perlite and coir peat in a large tub until the elements are thoroughly mixed.

Use propagation mix for:

- Offsets and runners (see page 244)
- Stem cuttings (see page 248)
- Petiole leaf cuttings (see page 252)
- Sectional leaf cuttings (see page 256)

LIGHT MIX

When you want to hang a plant on a wall or suspend a pot from the ceiling, it helps to use a potting mix that's lighter in weight than regular mix for ease of handling and safety. A light mix really comes into its own when you need to use removable hooks to fasten your hanging pots to walls and ceilings (see page 196).

Another option is sphagnum moss: a lightweight material that also acts as a perfect medium to pot numerous plants in. The great thing about sphagnum moss is that it not only makes the pot even lighter, but it also holds moisture for about twice as long, reducing the need to water hanging plants as frequently. The moss holds together well, too, which means you can water without mix washing out of the pot onto the floor or your furniture. Look for moss that is sustainably sourced – this will be listed on the bag.

YOU WILL NEED:

- 2 parts premium potting mix
- 2 parts perlite
- 1 part peat moss or coir peat

In a large tub, mix the potting mix, perlite and peat moss or coir peat together until the three ingredients are thoroughly blended.

Use light mix for:

- Arrowhead plant (*Syngonium*)
- Bromeliads (such as *Aechmea*, *Guzmania*, *Vriesea*)
- Jungle cacti (*Rhipsalis*, *Epiphyllum*)
- Moth orchid (*Phalaenopsis*)
- Philodendrons
- Pothos (*Epipremnum aureum*)
- Rhaphidophoras
- Swiss cheese vine (*Monstera adansonii*)
- Wax plant (*Hoya*)

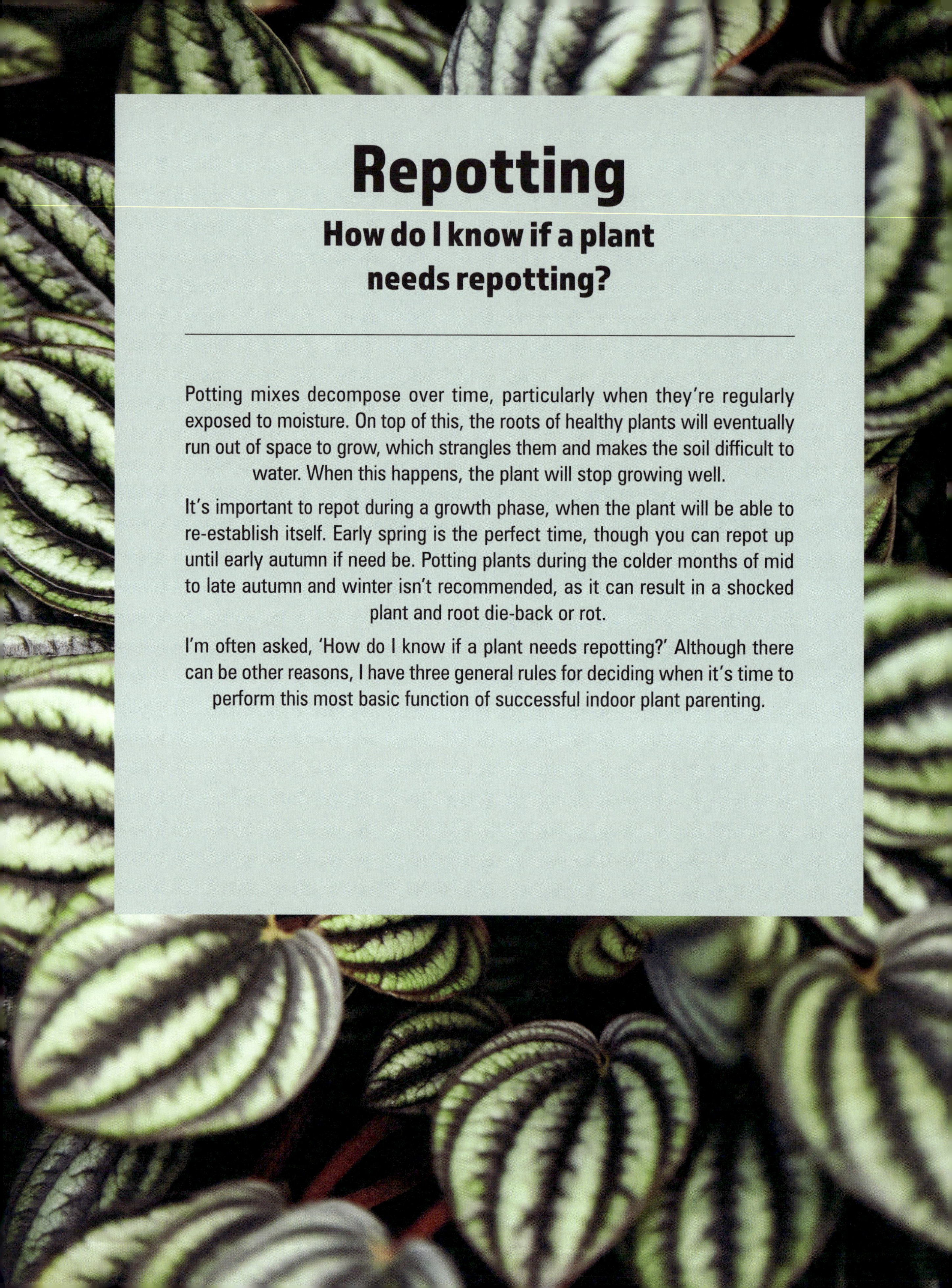

Repotting

How do I know if a plant needs repotting?

Potting mixes decompose over time, particularly when they're regularly exposed to moisture. On top of this, the roots of healthy plants will eventually run out of space to grow, which strangles them and makes the soil difficult to water. When this happens, the plant will stop growing well.

It's important to repot during a growth phase, when the plant will be able to re-establish itself. Early spring is the perfect time, though you can repot up until early autumn if need be. Potting plants during the colder months of mid to late autumn and winter isn't recommended, as it can result in a shocked plant and root die-back or rot.

I'm often asked, 'How do I know if a plant needs repotting?' Although there can be other reasons, I have three general rules for deciding when it's time to perform this most basic function of successful indoor plant parenting.

1 If you have recently bought a new plant to add to your home and it's during the growing season, I recommend you repot it in one of the mixes listed here in this chapter as soon as is practical. The reason behind this is that the composition of potting mixes used by commercial growers is often not great for home care – it is geared towards encouraging plants to grow as fast and as cheaply as possible to get them into the marketplace to sell. Setting up your plant in one of the potting mixes you have made yourself will give it the head start it needs to thrive in your care.

2 Look at the size of the plant versus the size of the pot. If the plant is a lot larger than the pot, it's time to have a look at the roots. The best way to do this is to take the plant to a spot where you can gently remove it from the pot to see if there are too many roots in there. If it's in a plastic pot, start by feeling the outside: is the pot very firm? The more roots there are, the firmer the pot will feel. Now gently pull the plant out; as you do this, you will be able to see if it's root bound or not. Root binding is easy to see: there will be lots of tangled roots winding round and round with little space for soil. However, if lots of soil starts to fall out and you can't see many roots, gently place the plant back in the pot and give it some more time to fill out before repotting.

3 How long has a plant been in the same pot? To help you answer this question, it's a good idea to buy those little white labels you can find at your local plant store. Write the date that you repotted or bought the plant on a label, stick it in the pot and it will save you needing to remember, which becomes especially hard once you have more than a few plants … life's busy, who remembers this stuff? If it's been in the same container for a couple of years, it will benefit from having fresh soil and a general tidy-up.

TIP:

If you don't like the look of labels, write the date on the side of the pot. Use a contrasting permanent marker for plastic pots and a grey lead pencil for clay pots.

How to

REPOT A PLANT

You've worked out that your plant has outgrown its pot, but how to go about repotting it without damaging the plant and to give it the best chance of thriving? Here are the steps I always take, and once you've done it a few times, you'll realise just how simple it is. Make it easier for yourself by clearing space on a work surface and getting out all of your equipment before you start. It also makes sense to check all of your plants and repot any that require it in the one session. Your plants will thank you for it and repay you with new growth and good health.

YOU WILL NEED:

- Plant for repotting
- Bench or firm surface to work on
- Plastic nursery pot
- Hand trowel
- Potting mix appropriate for your chosen plant
- Controlled-release fertiliser pellets
- Watering can or hose with a soft-spray attachment

YOU MAY ALSO NEED:

- Gardening gloves
- Old butter knife
- Old chopstick or teaspoon
- Secateurs
- Seaweed solution

1

2

3

1 Gently squeeze the plastic pot to loosen the soil and roots. If your plant is in terracotta or another firm pot, you may need to run a butter knife around the inside edge of the pot; you can also push a blunt object into the drainage hole to dislodge the root ball. Extremely pot-bound plants might need heavy duty intervention – sometimes you have no alternative but to crack open a clay pot or cut a plastic one to remove the plant.

2 Once the plant is loose, hold the base of the trunk, stems or branches and slowly lift the plant out of the pot. I always feel around the plant first to gauge how delicate it is and the best place to hold it to avoid damaging it. Don't be hard on yourself if a few leaves or stems break off! While some plants are tough as old leather, other plants are very fragile. After you've repotted a few different types of plants, you will start to feel more confident with this.

TIP:

If a plant is very root bound or it seems like pulling it upwards out of the pot will result in damage, lie the loosened pot on its side and gently shake or massage the pot with one hand while easing the plant out with the other.

3 Carefully loosen the roots so that the soil falls away and the roots are freed from the main root ball. Try not to break off too many roots, although sometimes this is unavoidable. If the roots are very tightly wound, you will need to be a bit firmer. Use a chopstick or the handle of a teaspoon to gently tease out the outer roots so that when they go into the new pot they will grow more quickly outward into the fresh soil. I give the plant a light shake at this stage to remove any loose mix and roots. This is also a great time to inspect the roots: healthy roots are generally firm and pale in colour with pale, active growing tips, although some plants can have roots of a different colour (such as reddish or dark brown). Dark, mushy roots are generally a sign of rot, while dry, brown roots that have no moisture inside when cut are dead. Both of these should be removed with secateurs.

4 The plant is now ready to go into its new pot. If the plant is healthy and there are lots of roots in the pot, a larger pot will be of benefit and encourage new growth. If the pot is only half full of roots and a lot of soil falls out when you remove it, it's better to use a pot of the same size as the one the plant came out of, and you will simply replace the old soil with fresh. Some plants like snug roots, while others like lots of soil to grow into – for the lowdown on a particular plant's next-level care, I encourage you to research the plant in question. As a general rule, I usually pot up to the next size nursery pot, unless I know a particular plant is a fast grower.

5 Place some potting mix in the new pot, enough so that when you hold the plant in the centre of the pot the base is a couple of centimetres below the rim and the roots are touching the mix in the bottom. The ideal position for a plant to sit is with the roots covered but the trunk, stem or stems above the soil line. Generally the position a plant is in when you buy it from the nursery is about right, so try to aim for that.

TIP:

If you have a pot with large drainage holes from which soil is escaping, coffee filters make a great barrier, keeping the soil in the pot but allowing water to drain through. Just place them over the holes before adding mix to the pot.

6 Next fill around the roots with potting mix using a trowel or your hand. Keep filling until the mix reaches the desired level, then grab the pot with both hands and firmly tap it a few times on the surface. If there are areas where the soil has sunk, add more mix and then tap again. Don't press the soil down because this can remove pockets of air that are good for the roots.

7 Now sprinkle over the controlled-release fertiliser pellets (refer to the packet for the recommended dosage). These little spheres control the amount of nutrients that your plant receives depending on the temperature and moisture levels. Some people mix them into the soil but I prefer using them as a top dressing so I don't forget that I've applied it – I can see how old they are and know when to reapply. For more information on fertilising, see page 146.

8 Finally, give the plant a good drink. Water the pot until water runs out of the drainage holes. Then drain it well before moving it to its new home.

TIP:

I use a half-strength seaweed solution to water in my newly potted plants. It gives them a boost during a time of stress. Simply use a watering can to apply the seaweed solution generously to the soil and leaves.

‘If the plant is healthy and there are lots of roots in the pot, a larger pot will be of benefit and encourage new growth.’

Containers

What should I grow my plants in?

Like all of us, indoor plants need something to grow in and call home. As well as holding the potting mix, the pot you choose will contribute greatly to the success you have in growing a plant. Plus, let's not forget that the pot plays a big role in how a plant looks in your home.

Plastic nursery pots

It's plastic pots hands down for me. They're light and easy to move around, hold onto moisture for longer than terracotta or clay pots, and they also drain well. They're cheap and you can clean and reuse them. If they don't fit into a decorative pot, just get out the scissors and 'snip snip snip' to cut them down! Why do people think you can't cut down a $2 plastic pot? I cut down big plastic pots to make wide, shallow ones for plants that are shallow rooted, like peperomias and goeppertias. A plastic pot also makes it easy to feel the roots and firmness of the soil, something that's very helpful when you are deciding if a plant needs to be repotted. One of the other reasons I use plastic pots is their portability, as I like to move my plants regularly between different decorative planters and positions. Plastic pots also have matching saucers in every size that can be used inside a decorative planter or under the pot wherever it's sitting.

I recommend clear pots, if you can find them. I really don't know why they are not more popular. For me they're perfect because you can actually see the roots and diagnose any problems without disturbing the plant – it's like having X-ray vision. It's also immensely satisfying to see healthy roots start to appear through the sides as the plant establishes itself.

Decorative pots (ceramic, plastic, metal etc.)

I'm a decorative pot hoarder. I think I love them almost as much as I love my plants, BUT I don't think they're suitable for growing in directly. Some are porous and some aren't, some have drainage holes and some don't – it's way too variable. It's also highly likely that a container exposed to soil and moisture for an extended period of time is going to be damaged by staining, rusting, cracking or even breakage, and quite often the shape makes it very difficult or impossible to remove a root bound plant without smashing or cutting the planter.

Another reason I don't plant directly into decorative pots is that moving my plants from pot to pot in different groupings brings me so much joy! Why commit a plant to one look for an extended length of time? It's so much fun to style your plants up in differently shaped or coloured vessels whenever you feel like it. Pots are often quite heavy as well, so to lift and move the plant to water it or treat a pest can be a real chore. To me, decorative pots are more suited to sheathing over the top of an internal plastic pot, which can be removed or changed at will.

If your decorative planter has no drainage hole but you just can't get your head around plonking a plastic pot inside it, buy a plastic pot plant saucer that fits as closely as possible into the base of the pot and turn it upside down. Position it at the bottom of the planter and then pot up your plant as usual. The saucer will give you a section of air around 2 cm high under the roots where water can drain away – this will help you avoid overwatering, one of the main problems you will face with no drainage holes.

TIP:

I keep small plastic food containers that things like desserts and dips are packaged in to use as round pots for small stylish planters such as porcelain cups, soup bowls and even little vases. All you need to do is cut a small drainage hole in the bottom and trim the top with scissors so it fits perfectly inside without being seen.

Terracotta pots

Personally, I don't like terracotta pots. It's such a porous material and it constantly draws moisture out of the soil, leaching out nutrients as well. It's not a stable, predictable environment for your plants' roots to thrive in. Terracotta is also heavy and when my plants start needing larger pots they are not as portable as I like them to be.

I think terracotta looks great, so why not treat this type of pot as a decorative planter by placing a plastic-potted plant inside it? If you really want to plant directly into a terracotta pot, push a thin kitchen sponge into the base of the pot or paint the inside with clay pot sealer. The sponge will retain moisture and also prevent soil falling out of the drainage hole, and the sealer will make the terracotta less porous.

'Plastic pots are the best containers for your plants – they are cheap, light and easy to reuse. And if they don't fit into a decorative pot, just get out the scissors and cut them down!'

LIGHT & LOCATION

Why is light so important for plants?

So, you just fell in love with a plantastic specimen at your local plant shop and had to have it. You get it home and the big question now is: where will it live? Plants come from a broad variety of natural environments – luckily for us they are masters at adaptation, and we don't need to replicate steamy rainforests or sun-parched deserts to grow most plants successfully indoors. However, we do need to do our best to ensure that they are getting at least their basic requirements of light, temperature and humidity. It's an holistic approach to plant care: the more factors you can get right, the better your plants will respond and the more they will thrive. A plant that's receiving the right amount of daily light is well on its way to becoming a star specimen.

Plants use light to convert water, carbon dioxide and minerals into energy to grow, and release oxygen as a by-product. The miracle of nature called photosynthesis not only powers your house plants but also powers most of the world's ecosystems. Without adequate light, plants suffer from a form of starvation; light starved, they become weak, unable to grow properly and thrive, and are far more sensitive to other factors, such as temperature and humidity. Like any organism that has been weakened through a lack of essential nutrition, they are also more prone to disease and vulnerable to insect pests that further attack their health and vitality.

Plants need light or they die, and they have developed ingenious ways of getting more of the stuff – some perch high in a tree to reach the sun; most turn their leaves towards the light to expose the largest surface area to its life-giving rays; and yet others develop pigments and patterns that enable them to utilise even the smallest amounts of light, such as the sun-specks on a forest floor. At the other end of the spectrum are species endemic to high altitudes and parched deserts that cover themselves in sun-reflective scales or hairs to reflect the harshest rays, or have developed ingenious outer layers that keep precious moisture from evaporating during the heat of the day but open at night to absorb moisture in the air. Many of the plants suited to growing indoors come from the tropics, from rainforests where there are distinct areas with different levels of light: the canopy, right up the top where the sun is strongest; the mid-level, which has dappled shade; and the understorey, or forest floor, with its low light or full shade. When choosing a spot for a particular plant, I imagine my home and its various naturally lit areas as a mini rainforest with the same kinds of different microclimates and light levels.

What are the different types of indoor light?

Direct light, bright filtered light, indirect light; part shade, some sun, morning sun, sunny position … plant-care labels come in a language all of their own and each one is different. Have you ever thought, 'I have no idea what they're talking about'? Me too! It took me a long time to get a handle on the correct light requirements for indoor plants, but I can save you some of that time and effort by simplifying the jargon.

Indoor light can be divided into four types:

- **Direct light**
  aka some direct sun, morning sun, bright direct light, sunny position
- **Bright filtered light**
  aka bright indirect light, indirect light, bright light, morning sun, light position
- **Medium light**
  aka semi-shade, dappled light, shaded position
- **Low light**
  aka shade, full shade, dark position

You may have noticed that I don't include a category for direct afternoon sun, and that's because there are very few house plants that will tolerate this type of light coming directly through glass, other than some desert cacti and succulents. Direct afternoon sun can be harsh, especially when it's shining through clear glass and accompanied by infrared and UV rays or heat, which can build up quickly when the sun streams through a window. I have ruined plants by moving them for just a couple of hours from a low-light position to a spot close to a window in direct sun. Even cacti can be damaged by direct afternoon sun. While sunburnt plants might not die, sun damage is unsightly and can scar your beautiful specimens permanently. Plants also dehydrate very quickly in this position and some will need watering every day to prevent heat stress. So, for me, direct light means direct morning light from sunrise until about 1 pm, or progressively earlier the further north you're located.

There are some unfussy, easy-growing plants that do well in different types of light. For example, pothos (*Epipremnum aureum*) will look its best at the brighter end of the spectrum, but also does well in lower light. The lists on the following pages generally show the optimal light for each plant, but for the full range they will grow in, see the A–Z of indoor plants on page 15.

TIP:
Windows that face north or north-east provide the best position because they get the most sunlight throughout the day, especially in winter when the sun is at its lowest. Plants at a west-facing window need to be set well back from the glass, especially in summer.

How can I tell if a plant is getting enough light?

Plants that receive a good amount of light are compact, have stems that are strong and upright and leaves that are healthy and bright in colour, and new growth is present. Overall the plant will be increasing in size, and often the individual leaves will too. Move that plant to a spot where the light it's receiving is insufficient and the plant's stems will begin to elongate towards the light. This is called etiolation, and it's a survival mechanism whereby the plant searches out the life-giving sun (by the way, the word 'etiolate' always impresses plant people … try it and see!). It's also highly likely that any new leaves will be smaller and paler and old leaves may begin to yellow and die as the plant tries to reduce the amount of foliage it needs to support. Eventually the plant will be a shadow of its former self – weak and starved of energy, it will be prone to insect and fungal infestations and may die. Next time you're at a nursery see if you can find a group of the same type of plant where some are in the shade while others aren't. It's fun to observe the difference, and it can be really surprising how much low-light levels affect the overall condition of plants.

TIP:

When judging how much light is coming into a room, remember to look at whether the window is shaded by trees or eaves – this can have a big impact on available light.

To help you work out what type of light the plants will be getting at your place, here are some general guidelines based on the aspect of windows in the Southern Hemisphere.

- **North-facing windows**
  Direct light, bright filtered light
- **East-facing windows**
  Morning sun, direct light to bright filtered light
- **South-facing windows**
  No direct sun, medium light to some bright filtered light
- **West-facing windows**
  Direct afternoon sun to bright filtered light

‘When choosing a spot for a particular plant, I imagine my home and its various naturally lit areas as a mini rainforest with the same kinds of different microclimates and light levels.’

DIRECT LIGHT

Direct light is the morning or afternoon sunlight that shines through a window for about 1–1.5 m directly onto your plants. Direct morning sun is great for most light-loving plants as it's softer than the harsh rays of the afternoon sun, which can be damaging. It's important to remember that when sun shines through a window it dissipates quite quickly, so what is direct morning sun becomes bright filtered, medium and then low light the further you move away from the window.

TIP:

You can download free plant light meters onto your smartphone that will give you a very accurate idea of light levels at any given time. After using these for a while, you will find it becomes second nature to gauge your indoor jungle's light.

Plants suited to direct light

- Alocasias
- Angel wings (*Caladium*)
- Banana plant (*Musa*)
- Caudiciforms (such as *Fockea edulis*)
- Cordylines
- Desert cacti, including old man cacti
- Desert rose (*Adenium*)
- Dracaenas, including snake plant (*Dracaena trifasciata*)
- Elephant foot plant (*Dioscorea elephantipes*)
- English ivy (*Hedera helix*)
- Fiddle-leaf fig (*Ficus lyrata*)
- Geraniums
- Jungle cacti (*Rhipsalis*, *Epiphyllum*)
- Madagascar palm (*Pachypodium lamerei*)
- Ponytail palm (*Beaucarnea recurvata*)
- Succulents (most varieties)
- Vanda orchid
- Yuccas

BRIGHT FILTERED LIGHT

This is the goldilocks zone for most plants – it's where the light is just right. Many indoor plants do very well in this zone so you'll want to find long-term positions for most of your plants here if possible.

Bright filtered light is the type of light that shines between 20 cm and 1.5 m through a window that gets little direct sun but still has lots of natural light coming through it, or that you'll find 1–3 m back from a very sunny window. Direct light from a window that gets full afternoon sun can be softened to create bright filtered light by hanging a sheer curtain to break up the sun's rays. In horticultural greenhouses we use shade cloth to achieve this effect, and the idea here is the same – you're using a screen to reduce the amount of sun that hits your plants. Be careful, though: an existing sheer curtain may or may not significantly reduce the light, so experiment a bit before sitting your prized beauties in this position.

I place newly acquired plants in a spot that receives bright filtered light to acclimatise them to the light levels in my home. In the nursery, plants are usually grown under shade and the sudden shock of being moved into bright light can burn foliage, even if the plant is suited to those conditions. This is also something to keep in mind if you want to move plants you have had in lower light for a while to a new position. Slowly introduce them to bright light over a week or two by gradually moving them towards their new home.

TIP:

To protect plants from the extremes of burning sun during the day and rapid cooling overnight, never put plants so close to a window that their leaves are touching the glass. A general rule is a minimum of 10 cm from a shady window in mild conditions and at least 30 cm in colder or hotter seasons.

Plants suited to bright filtered light

- African violet (*Saintpaulia ionantha*)
- Alocasias
- Anthuriums
- Arrowhead plant (*Syngonium*)
- Begonias
- Bird of paradise (*Strelitzia*)
- Bird's nest anthurium (*Anthurium hookeri*)
- Bird's nest fern (*Asplenium nidus*)
- Bromeliads (such as *Aechmea*, *Guzmania*, *Neoregelia*, *Vriesea*)
- Chinese money plant (*Pilea peperomioides*)
- Coleus
- Cycads, including Chestnut dioon (*Dioon edule*)
- Cyclamen
- Dracaenas, including snake plant (*Dracaena trifasciata*) and dragon tree (*Dracaena marginata*)
- Dumb cane (*Dieffenbachia*)
- Fernleaf cacti (*Selenicereus chrysocardium*)
- Ferns (most varieties)
- Grape ivy (*Cissus rhombifolia*)
- Kentia palm (*Howea forsteriana*)
- Moth orchid (*Phalaenopsis*)
- Parlour palm (*Chamaedorea elegans*)
- Peperomias
- Pileas
- Prayer plants (*Ctenanthe*, *Goeppertia*, *Maranta*, *Stromanthe*)
- Purple shamrock (*Oxalis triangularis*)
- Rik-rak cacti (*Disocactus anguliger*)
- Rubber plant (*Ficus elastica*)
- Sago palm (*Cycas revoluta*)
- Spiderwort (*Tradescantia*)
- String of hearts (*Ceropegia woodii*)
- String of pearls (*Senecio rowleyanus*)
- Swiss cheese plant (*Monstera deliciosa*)
- Umbrella plant (*Schefflera*)
- Wax plant (*Hoya*)
- Zebra plant (*Haworthiopsis fasciata*)

‘A plant that’s receiving the right amount of daily light is well on its way to becoming a star specimen.’

MEDIUM LIGHT

Any spot that receives very little or no direct sun and that is further back from a window is where you'll find medium light: this will be 2–3 m from a sunny window and 1–2 m from a bright window that has no direct sun streaming through it. This is the zone where most people put the majority of their plants, because it tends to be smack bang in the middle of their living areas where there are surfaces like coffee tables, bathroom vanities and kitchen benches.

Because medium light is not the goldilocks zone for all plants, we need to be more careful about what kinds of plants we place here to ensure they thrive. No need to worry – there are still loads of potential occupants. Plants that like bright filtered light will also do okay here: the list below includes a few select plants that prefer a brighter spot but will tolerate medium light well.

TIP:

I get it, you want that special plant that loves bright filtered light on the coffee table where it looks amazing! Go ahead, I support you – but make a plan to let it sit there for a month or so and then move it back to a well-lit position, swapping it out for another stunner that's had a spell drinking in the sun. This works wonders all over the house, and I've been doing it for years with great results … even with cacti!

Plants suited to medium light

- Air plants (*Tillandsia*)
- Chinese evergreens (*Aglaonema*)
- Elkhorn fern (*Platycerium bifurcatum*)
- Flamingo flower plant (*Anthurium andraeanum*)
- Japanese aralia (*Fatsia japonica*)
- Jewel orchids (*Macodes*, *Ludisia*)
- Ming aralia (*Polyscias*)
- Nerve plant (*Fittonia*)
- Philodendrons
- Pileas
- Prayer plants (*Goeppertia*, *Maranta*)
- Rhaphidophoras
- Rubber plant (*Ficus elastica*)
- Satin pothos (*Scindapsus pictus*)
- Spider plant (*Chlorophytum comosum*)
- Swiss cheese plant (*Monstera deliciosa*)
- Watermelon vine (*Pellionia*)
- Wax plant (*Hoya*)
- Weeping fig (*Ficus benjamina*)

LOW LIGHT

Low light is found in any position more than 1–3 m from a window, depending on the window's aspect. There are many areas in our homes that fall into this category and it creates one of the biggest challenges for indoor gardeners, judging by one of the questions I'm asked the most: 'What plants are good for low-light areas?'

While most indoor plants can't survive in low light for extended periods of time, there are some hardy survivors that will. If you only have low-light options in your home and don't want to be limited to plants that tolerate these conditions, you could consider buying grow lights. These are LEDs that are purpose built to produce the red and violet light that plants use to grow, and advances in technology mean they're reasonably cheap to buy.

TIP:

The dust and grime that build up on a window and a plant's leaves have a big impact on how much light a plant absorbs. It's good plant practice to clean windows near plants before spring and again in autumn. Leaves will benefit from a regular shower under a spray nozzle to dislodge dust. If you don't have a spray nozzle, a sponge dampened with lukewarm water works wonders.

Plants suited to low light

- Cast iron plant (*Aspidistra*)
- Chinese evergreens (*Aglaonema*)
- Dragon tail (*Rhaphidophora decursiva*)
- Happy plant (*Dracaena fragrans*)
- Lady palm (*Rhapis excelsa*)
- Parlour palm (*Chamaedorea elegans*)
- Peace lily (*Spathiphyllum*)
- Philodendrons
- Pothos (*Epipremnum aureum*)
- Snake plant (*Dracaena trifasciata*)
- Spider plant (*Chlorophytum comosum*)
- ZZ plant (*Zamioculcas zamiifolia*)

‘I get it, you want that special plant that loves bright light to sit on the coffee table where it looks amazing. Go ahead, put it there, but make sure you move it back to a well-lit position after a month or so.’

WATERING & FERTILISING

Mastering the art of watering

Plants need water the same way that we humans do. Much of their structure contains water and they use it along with minerals and sunlight to produce energy to grow. Plants have evolved in their natural environments to utilise water both in its liquid form, as rain, and as a gas in the form of vapour or humidity in the air, so where a plant comes from dictates what kind of moisture levels it needs. In the home environment, plants are completely dependent on you to give them the precious H_2O that they require to flourish.

More than any other area of plant care, watering causes the most grief for people, and it's easy to understand why. Water too much and your plants will quickly weaken and die; water too little and the same thing will happen. When the soil becomes waterlogged, water fills the spaces where air would usually be, encouraging bacteria that rot the roots and essentially suffocating the plant. If a plant doesn't receive enough water it simply dehydrates, stops growing in an effort to conserve moisture and eventually keels over in protest.

But the good news is that it's actually not that hard to get it right. Surprisingly, it's one of the easiest areas to master, especially if you don't mind getting your hands dirty – well, your fingertip to be exact. The key to watering any plant properly is learning to monitor the moisture in the soil by the way the potting mix looks and feels: moist to wet soil appears darker and feels cooler, while dry soil looks lighter and greyer in tone and feels warmer.

The trick is to dip your fingertip into the top layer of potting mix to get a clear idea of what it looks and feels like 1–3 cm down. Using this method is fast, efficient and accurate. You can wear gloves if you prefer – you'll still be able to feel the moisture in the soil wearing the thinner latex type, though gardening gloves will only allow you to see the colour of the soil – but for me nothing beats touching the soil directly (then again, I've had my hands in the dirt since I was a four-year-old). It's important to dip into the potting mix because the surface dries quite quickly and relying on sight alone is not enough to accurately judge if a plant needs watering or not.

If you want to avoid the fingertip method altogether, you can use a soil moisture meter instead. There are a few different types available, including portable ones that you can move from pot to pot and fixed ones that stay with one plant. The downside of these meters is that measuring with the former is slow and investing in the latter is expensive, especially when you have more than a few plants. It's also difficult to gauge how deep you are inserting the meter into a pot, especially if the pot is large. I have found them inaccurate and gimmicky in the past, although the technology appears to be getting better. Still, for me, the human touch wins hands down, and I encourage you to try it first.

Why can't I just water once a week?

Why is monitoring the moisture of the soil in indoor pot plants important? Why can't we simply water all of them once a week? Well, plants don't need the same amount of water all year round – in fact, their water needs can vary from week to week and month to month. Factors such as whether the plant is actively growing and the temperature and humidity levels will have a big impact on a plant's water needs. This is why it's a big mistake to have a regular watering day when you water every plant regardless of the moisture level of the soil.

Many (though not all) indoor plants tend to grow during the warmer months, and this is when a plant's needs, combined with higher temperatures and longer daylight hours, mean it will require more frequent watering. As the weather cools, growth slows down and the plant will use less water. Air conditioning and heating also have an impact: they dry the air in your home, contributing to evaporation of water from the plant and pot. The effect that all of these ambient and climatic conditions have on your plants' water needs can be easily managed by monitoring the soil, because the moisture level in the soil is what matters when it comes to deciding when to water.

How often should I water my plants?

Different kinds of plants have different water requirements: some like to be drier, some prefer constant moisture and some are more forgiving and accept a range of moisture levels. As a start, to help me give my plants the water they need, I place them into one of the three categories opposite as a general guide for how often I water them. I've placed plants in their optimal watering category, but some will still thrive with a bit less or a bit more – see the A–Z of indoor plants on page 15 for more information on each plant. When you buy a plant, or if one of your plants is not performing as well as you would like, I encourage you to research its water requirements – drilling down into the details of its water needs will pay off in spades. It's also important to pay close attention to the appearance of your plants and learn to recognise the signs of possible over- and underwatering.

Low water needs (water sparingly)

These plants do best when the soil is allowed to dry out completely between waterings.

- Bird of paradise (*Strelitzia*)
- Chinese money plant (*Pilea peperomioides*)
- Copper spoons (*Kalanchoe orgyalis*)
- Desert cacti, including old man cacti
- Elkhorn fern (*Platycerium bifurcatum*)
- Hens and chicks (*Echeveria*)
- Madagascar palm (*Pachypodium lamerei*)
- Moth orchid (*Phalaenopsis*)
- Ox tongue plant (*Gasteria*)
- Ponytail palm (*Beaucarnea recurvata*)
- Rubber plant (*Ficus elastica*)
- Snake plant (*Dracaena trifasciata*)
- String of hearts (*Ceropegia woodii*)
- String of pearls (*Senecio rowleyanus*)
- Zebra plant (*Haworthiopsis fasciata*)
- ZZ plant (*Zamioculcas zamiifolia*)

Moderate water needs (keep moist but not wet)

These plants love it when the soil is allowed to dry out about 2–4 cm deep before rewatering.

- African violet (*Saintpaulia ionantha*)
- Air plants (*Tillandsia*)
- Alocasias
- Angel wings (*Caladium*)
- Anthuriums
- Arrowhead plant (*Syngonium*)
- Begonias
- Bird's nest fern (*Asplenium nidus*)
- Bromeliads (such as *Aechmea*, *Guzmania*, *Neoregelia*, *Vriesea*)
- Caudiciforms (such as *Fockea edulis*)
- Chinese evergreens (*Aglaonema*)
- Coleus
- Cycads, such as chestnut dioon (*Dioon edule*)
- Cyclamen
- Dumb cane (*Dieffenbachia*)
- Elephant foot plant (*Dioscorea elephantipes*)
- English ivy (*Hedera helix*)
- Fernleaf cacti (*Selenicereus chrysocardium*)
- Fiddle-leaf fig (*Ficus lyrata*)
- Flamingo flower plant (*Anthurium andraeanum*)
- Grape ivy (*Cissus rhombifolia*)
- Happy plant (*Dracaena fragrans*)
- Jungle cacti (*Rhipsalis*)
- Kentia palm (*Howea forsteriana*)
- Peace lily (*Spathiphyllum*)
- Peperomias
- Philodendrons
- Pothos (*Epipremnum aureum*)
- Prayer plant (*Goeppertia, Maranta*)
- Purple shamrock (*Oxalis triangularis*)
- Rhaphidophoras
- Rik-rak cacti (*Disocactus anguliger*)
- Satin pothos (*Scindapsus pictus*)
- Spider plant (*Chlorophytum comosum*)
- Spiderwort (*Tradescantia*)
- Swiss cheese plant (*Monstera deliciosa*)
- Umbrella plant (*Schefflera*)
- Vanda orchid
- Wax plant (*Hoya*)

High water needs (keep constantly moist)

These plants thrive when you allow the soil to dry out about 1–2 cm deep before rewatering.

- Baby's tears (*Soleirolia soleirolii*)
- Boston fern (*Nephrolepis exaltata*)
- Club moss (*Selaginella*)
- Elephant ears (*Colocasia*)
- Maidenhair fern (*Adiantum*)
- Nerve plant (*Fittonia*)
- Peacock plant (*Goeppertia orbifolia*)
- Pitcher plants (*Nepenthes*)

TIP:

The size of a plant's pot makes a difference as to when it's the right time to water – the larger the pot, the deeper the soil needs to dry out. For example, if a plant with moderate water requirements is in a small, 12 cm pot, let it dry out to a depth of about 2 cm before watering it; however, if it is in a 25 cm pot, let it dry out 4 cm deep before watering.

‘Go ahead, share the shower with your plants! It’s the perfect place to water indoors, especially for plants that are too big to fit in the kitchen sink.’

SIGNS OF OVERWATERING

· wet soil
· weak, fragile growth
· wilting (due to loss of roots)
· rotting stems
· black spots on the leaves
· yellowing leaves
· leaf drop

Trickily, these symptoms can also be signs of other issues, so if you don't think you have been watering the plant too much and the soil isn't too wet, then it's highly likely it's not overwatering that's causing the problems (see Pests and Diseases, page 165).

If you discover a beloved plant has been sitting in water or has waterlogged soil, here is what to do. Grab an old towel and wrap it around the base of the pot, making sure to cover the drainage holes and arranging the towel in such a way that the pot will remain upright. Leave it for at least 12 hours. The towel will act as a wick, drawing the excess moisture out of the pot.

SIGNS OF UNDERWATERING

· wilting
· shrinking of leaves and stems
· curling leaves
· no growth
· yellowing leaves
· leaf drop
· browning leaf edges
· dulling of leaf colour

As with overwatering, it's possible that these symptoms are caused by other issues, but it's logical to rule out lack of water first. When you water soil that is very dry, the water will often run straight through without thoroughly re-wetting the potting mix – even though the top layer of soil will darken, giving the appearance that the plant has been watered properly. It's best to water the plant well, leave it for 20 minutes and then water it again. Alternatively, sit the pot in a shallow saucer of water, which will allow the soil to slowly absorb the liquid.

How and when should I water my plants?

First, use tepid water whenever possible. I'm not fond of cold showers and neither are indoor plants! So don't drench your plants with cold water if you can help it, and definitely don't do it in the cooler seasons.

Water each plant until water runs from the drainage holes – this is very important, and it might not be for the reason you think. We not only want to make sure that the mix is evenly watered but we also want the water running through the soil to draw fresh air down into the mix, as fresh air in pockets of the soil leads to healthy root systems. If you water in situ with a watering can it's not possible to give a plant a really good water because the saucer won't be able to catch all of the run-off. I recommend using a watering can for two or three waterings, and then every third or fourth time give them a really good soak at the sink.

When watering with a can, pour in enough to fill the top of the pot with a centimetre or so of water; wait for this to sink in before repeating once more. An hour or so later, work your way around again to empty any saucers that are full. Most plants that sit in water and slowly reabsorb the excess will suffer from too much of a good thing.

Each indoor plant has what's known as a 'water table' in its pot. This is a section of the lower potting mix that won't drain properly without help because of the effect of gravity. To give it a boost, pick the pot up and tilt it on an angle over the sink, then lift it up and down. You will find heaps of water will drain out that would otherwise sit in the soil and cause problems.

Many plants love water sprayed over their leaves, and as long as the weather is not cold it's a welcome tonic. It dislodges dust and also discourages pests like spider mites (see page 172) that have a particular hatred of wet leaves. If you're not sure if a plant likes having water on its leaves, do a little Google; however, most are happy for rain, even if it's artificial.

Finally, in terms of timing, water in the morning if you can. This gives enough time for the pot to adequately drain, the leaves to dry and the plant to use some of the water before the temperature drops in the evening.

TIP:

Turn a plastic nursery saucer upside down, place it inside a decorative pot that doesn't have drainage holes, then sit your inner pot on top of it. This ensures that the plant won't sit in run-off and become waterlogged. It's also a great way to position a smaller plant at the correct height inside a decorative pot.

Where should I water my plants?

When thinking about where to water your plants, you'll need to take into consideration the size of the plant and its pot, when the plant last had a really good water and how much time you have. If you are lucky enough to have a balcony, courtyard or backyard, these are great locations to give plants a proper drenching in the warmer months. However, if you don't have those outdoor spaces, here are the three places I water most of my indoor plants.

At the kitchen sink

My kitchen sink has an extendable hose with a shower attachment that is perfect for watering pot plants. I use the sink when I want to give a plant a good soak so there's lots of water running out of the pot, when I want to wet a plant that is growing over a totem and when I want to give a small- or medium-sized plant a shower.

TIP:

You can buy metal and rubber mats or steel grates that fit on top of your sink to turn it into an open work surface. These are excellent for watering and draining plants on. Depending on the size of your kitchen sink, a large wire cake rack can also work well.

In situ, with a watering can

It's helpful to have both a small 1.5 litre and a large 9 litre watering can. The large ones are great for watering a few plants at a time, while the small ones make it easy to get the spout into hard-to-reach areas and under the leaves of bushy plants. While it's convenient to water plants in situ, as I mentioned opposite, it's not good to do this all the time. It may be your only option if a plant is simply too large to move, but whenever possible try to water at the sink at least every third or fourth time until water is flowing well out of the drainage holes.

TIP:

Have an old bath towel or hand towel close by when you're watering, as it's almost impossible to water plants without some water splashing off the leaves or pot. This way you can clean up any drips straight away.

In the shower recess

I use the shower recess to water plants that are in need of a good soaking but are too big to fit in the sink. As long as you can lift them safely, it's the perfect place to drench a few plants at a time, especially if you have a hose with a shower fitting. Leave them for an hour or so to drain thoroughly before putting them back into place.

Water quality

There is a LOT of discussion among plant people about the pros and cons of watering with tap water. You may hear about a certain plant that hates chlorine or hard water or some other mineral present in tap water. Here's my two cents. I have always found tap water to be absolutely fine for nearly all of my plants – the only ones I treat differently are carnivorous plants. I choose distilled water for these because in their natural habitat they grow in materials that are virtually mineral free.

Chlorine levels in tap water are way below what is harmful for plants, so let's dispel that myth to start with. Water hardness, or the levels of calcium and magnesium in tap water, is more annoying than damaging – the harder the water, the more 'water marks' you will find on your leaves because tiny quantities of minerals are left behind if you spray the leaves regularly. My home in Bali has very hard water and I have as broad a selection of species there as I do in my Melbourne digs, but I have never had a problem with a plant not liking the water. If you're watering properly and caring for your plants by repotting them when they need it, I don't believe there is any reason to be worried about watering your plants with tap water in Australia.

‘Plants don’t just absorb nutrients and minerals through their roots, they also take them in above the ground. So when treating your plants, wet the leaves as well as the soil. This really peps them up!’

Fertilising

My fertilising regimen is simple. I use three types of fertiliser for my plants: controlled-release pellets, seaweed solution and liquid fertiliser. There are numerous brands of each type and you will find your favourites. The beauty of controlled-release fertiliser pellets is that the membrane surrounding the nutrients only allows the plant to be fed when the temperature is warm and when there is moisture present. This means you have little fertiliser robots sitting in the top of your potting mix, only feeding your plants when they need it … how cool is that?

There are a number of different formulations of fertiliser labelled for different plants. Although it might sound obvious, I use one labelled for indoor plants. I grow most of my plants for the beauty of their foliage, and some of the indoor formulations contain levels of certain minerals that promote flowering along with foliage. Despite this, I've achieved great results using the general-purpose formulas and can highly recommend them.

As well as the pelletised fertiliser, I use liquid tonics, too. I like seaweed solution the best because it's completely organic, very gentle on plant roots and leaves and has a host of minerals and trace elements to encourage growth. Apply it at the full dose recommended by the manufacturer for indoor plants; during the growing season apply it every two weeks on vigorously growing plants and every four weeks on slower growing plants. I also apply a liquid fertiliser at the same time as the seaweed solution by mixing it into the solution at half strength. I prefer liquid fertilisers with high nitrogen levels, because this encourages foliage growth.

Liquid food can be applied to the leaves and stems too: this is called foliar application. Plants don't just absorb nutrients and minerals through their roots – they also take them in via the tissue above the ground, so when you're treating your plants wet the leaves as well as the soil. This really peps them up! You can also water freshly planted cuttings with seaweed solution and again when they start to produce roots to get them growing as quickly as possible.

TIP:

Seaweed solution is a great tonic for stressed plants. In general, plants that have been sent by post or newly potted plants will benefit from a water with this mineral-rich liquid.

TEMPERATURE & HUMIDITY

Temperature

Light isn't the only factor to consider when deciding on your plants' location – the temperature of the air around them is also important. Many of the most popular indoor plants originated in the subtropics or wet tropics, and these environments generally have stable temperatures that aren't too cold or too hot. It's just as well we humans like similar temperatures, so you can be pretty sure that if you feel comfortable with the temperature in your home, your plants do, too.

There are two main temperature categories that I use: cool (15–22°C) and warm (17–28°C). While you can't cater to every plant with your indoor climate, it's good to know what a particular plant prefers when positioning it in your house. Luckily, most will do well somewhere in the middle of these two ranges. In the A–Z of indoor plants (see page 15), I give each plant's preferred temperatue; some plants can cope with a broader range and these are listed as 'cool to warm'.

Most indoor plants don't enjoy it once the thermometer drops below 15°C. I aim to keep temperatures above 18°C during the cooler months; below this, growth tends to slow right down. At the other end of the scale, temperatures over 33°C, especially for extended lengths of time, will put your plants under stress.

The general rule for temperature is to try to avoid rapid fluctuations and keep it as stable as possible. This is why draughts are often cited as being bad for our plants – they are usually cold air blowing in from outside. Windows are always cooler in winter, too, so don't put plants directly against them. Just as essential is keeping delicate plants away from heaters and air conditioners, because these not only create temperatures way out of a plant's natural comfort zone but also dry the air, reducing humidity – and that's a double whammy against happy plants.

'You can be pretty sure that if you feel comfortable with the temperature in your home, your plants do, too.'

How to

KEEP YOUR PLANTS COSY IN WINTER

If you find it a challenge to provide a cosy winter for your indoor garden, here is a hack I swear by that I use on my more temperamental tropical specimens with great success. This simple device will act as an insulating 'sock' that reduces the temperature fluctuation of the soil and keeps the roots warmer than the surrounding air. Not only will it help any delicate plants survive winter, but some plants will also continue growing when they would usually go into a cold-induced hibernation. It's deceptively simple but well worth the effort.

YOU WILL NEED:

- Scissors
- Bubble wrap, preferably with large bubbles, available from hardware and office supply stores
- Plant in plastic nursery pot
- Sticky tape
- Decorative pot

1 Cut a piece of bubble wrap, wrap it around the plant in its plastic nursery pot and tape the ends together.

2 Trim off any excess bubble wrap that is sitting above the rim of the plastic nursery pot or below the base.

3 Slip it into a decorative pot and you're done! Your plant will remain cosy throughout the cooler months.

How important is humidity?

The best humidity range for indoor plants seems to be one of the most hotly debated topics on plant forums and social media. There's no doubt that extra moisture in the air will have great benefits for the health and beauty of your plants, but sometimes high humidity is presented as the magic bullet for any tropical plant that doesn't seem to be thriving. I think it's a bit overrated, though, and I'll tell you why a little later.

First, let's chat about why plants like a specific humidity range in the first place. Plants breathe through pores in their leaves called stomata, and as part of this process they absorb and give off water vapour; this is an important part of photosynthesis, the basic function that sustains plant life. Plants have evolved to function best in their natural environments, so if a tropical plant is used to a warm jungle with high humidity, its leaves, stems and roots will have developed to work optimally under these conditions.

Take that humidity away and the tropical plant needs to work harder to grow: it will lose moisture from its leaves, which will become dull and develop dry edges; new leaves won't properly unfurl and older ones will yellow and drop sooner than they should; and growth overall will be slower and reduced. Conversely, many plants that originate in deserts or more arid environments enjoy lower moisture levels in the air and drier conditions generally, and will find very high humidity tough going. Luckily, though, you don't need to replicate a steamy rainforest or parched desert to grow fabulous indoor specimens. There are lots of plants that thrive in average humidity and even finnicky tropicals that will reward you with vitality and vigour with just a moderate increase of moisture in the air.

What is the ideal humidity for plants?

Let's look at the level of air humidity in most homes. The difference between the ideal humidity usually recommended for indoor plants and the humidity range that I have found actually works for the vast majority of them might surprise you. First and foremost, there's a reason why we don't live in tropical greenhouses, although that might seem like a great idea. Humidity of 70–80 per cent, which is the range often recommended for some popular indoor plants, is not workable in the average home. In reality, mouldy bed linen and windows covered in condensation are not most people's idea of comfort or healthy living. Above all, I believe our plants need to fit in with our day-to-day lives, not the other way around.

The humidity in a house will vary from climate to climate and season to season. Heating and air conditioning also affect humidity levels, but with a few tweaks, tools and tips we can supplement the humidity in our homes to strike the perfect balance for plants and people alike. The ideal indoor relative humidity range for people is 40–60 per cent. I have found the ideal range for plants is 50–60 per cent – most plants, including those from drier environments, are very happy indeed with 50–55 per cent, and only the more fussy tropical plants need the higher level. Within this range, you won't get the kind of growth in some tropical plants that you would achieve in a greenhouse or their natural environment, but it's worth remembering that in the tropics most plants grow very quickly. I view slower growth as a bonus rather than a downside, because who wants their specimens to outgrow their pots in only a few months?

TIP:

If you want to become a next-level plant parent, you can buy a digital hygrometer to measure the humidity in your home. At under $20, these are very affordable and are available from department and hardware stores as well as online. I have one that also contains a digital thermometer, which is uber practical. A hygrometer is not essential, though, and if you prefer you can rely instead on the way your plants are growing and how they respond to the tips over the page. In the end, a happy plant is the ultimate goal.

Tips for increasing humidity

Below I've created a little 'humidity resources' department to give you some ideas on how to boost the moisture in the air around your plants. It's worth the effort, and your plants will thank you for it with glistening, healthy leaves.

Humidifiers

Humidifiers are by far the best option for a larger plant collection or if, like me, you treat your plants as family members. A few years ago these were in my too-hard basket, as they were expensive and cumbersome. However, with the advent of ultrasonic humidifiers they are now affordable and widely available. I have two large domestic models, suitable for larger rooms, and I try to run at least one every day if I remember. They work a treat – I sit my more humidity-hungry plants closer to the unit, though all of my plants benefit from the increase in air moisture. I usually maintain about 50–60 per cent humidity, but I definitely don't panic if it drops below that for a week or so at a time. I also love the look of mist floating into the air and find it very calming. Ultrasonic humidifiers need regular cleaning every couple of weeks to keep them fresh and free of mineral build-up.

Gravel trays

Take a shallow, waterproof tray, fill it with a layer of small pebbles or gravel 1.5–3 cm deep, and then pour in water until it's just under the top of the medium. Sit your pots on top of this and as the water evaporates it will boost the humidity around the plants. For a single plant, a plastic nursery saucer will work well too, but a more elegant option is to fill a shallow ceramic bowl or large, deep platter with black or white pebbles and then sit a coordinating decorative planter on top. Gravel trays are a great solution for a few special plants, though they are not super practical for a larger collection. Plants that will benefit from the gravel tray treatment include the humidity-loving African violet (*Saintpaulia ionantha*), alocasias, club moss (*Selaginella*), crystal anthurium (*Anthurium crystallinum*), maidenhair fern (*Adiantum*) and moth orchid (*Phalaenopsis*).

TIP:

Shallow, wide pots increase the surface area of soil and as a result the ambient humidity under and around your plants. Cut down nursery pots with scissors and you'll find that these are great for lots of shallow-rooted jungle plants. Instead of potting a plant that's approximately 30 cm wide in a 15 × 15 cm standard pot, put it in a pot that's 25 cm wide and 7 cm deep. You'll get all that extra humidity under the plant without adding to the volume of mix.

Pot within a pot

This is one of my favourite methods because it's another bonus of growing your plants in plastic pots and sitting them inside larger, decorative pots that don't have drainage holes. Sit the inner pot on top of an upturned plastic saucer – or you can use a plastic container like the ones dips and yoghurt are sold in – to raise it a few centimetres off the bottom of the larger one. When you water, the runoff drains under the plant and then slowly evaporates, creating a microclimate around the plant. Just make sure that the pot itself isn't sitting in water, and every now and then pour out any water that's been sitting there for too long.

Misting

To mist or not to mist, that is the question. Is anyone else listening? Okay, I confess … I am a mister! I get a great deal of satisfaction from squeezing the trigger on my misting bottle and watching the thousands of glistening droplets fall gently onto the leaves of my eagerly awaiting plants (that is, I assume they're eager).

Misting indoor plants has gone through waves of popularity. In the 1970s and '80s it was touted as the trick to house plant mastery, then along came the 1990s and early 2000s and it was deemed a waste of time – and, even worse, was thought to encourage mould and fungal infections on your plants. The good news for us closet misters is that the research is now pointing the other way. It seems that the physical effect of tiny water droplets on the leaves actually strengthens the plant's immune system by activating a host of interesting chemicals.

I've been misting my plants on and off for many years and have found it beneficial in a number of ways: it does boost humidity, although only for a relatively short period; it discourages mites, the nemesis of most house plant hobbyists; and it acts as a tonic or pick-me-up for heat-stressed or dehydrated plants. It's also super useful for spraying onto the aerial roots of climbing plants to get them to fasten onto supports (more on that later in Maintenance, Grooming and Training, page 209).

If your plant collection is a modest size, any small misting bottle will be perfect for the job, whether it's made of plastic, glass or metal – there are many options available. A larger, pump-action pressure sprayer will take the hard work out of misting a lot of plants at the same time, and these are also perfect for applying fertiliser (see page 146) and insect sprays (see page 172). Misting a few times a week is plenty if you're supplementing the humidity levels in your home in other ways, but if the air is very dry, try misting twice a day (or more if you want). A light spray across each leaf of a plant is all that's needed; the leaves don't need to be completely wet. It's also beneficial to spray underneath the leaves and around the stems every few times as a way of discouraging the hell out of those spider mites. So try misting and see how it works for you! A word of warning: don't mist your plants when it's cold, as the water will sit on the leaves longer than it should, and it's then that fungal problems can occur.

Terrariums

Growing plants in enclosed or semi-enclosed glass containers is super cool right now, but terrariums have been used for centuries as a great way to grow smaller and more difficult plants that need very high humidity and constant moisture. This includes plants like jewel orchids (*Ludisia discolor*, *Macodes petola*), nerve plants (*Fittonia*), club moss (*Selaginella*) and carnivorous plants such as the Venus flytrap (*Dionaea muscipula*) and smaller pitcher plants (*Nepenthes*). They all thrive under these conditions and you can create mini junglescapes that will fascinate you and your visitors. See page 201 for how to create a terrarium-like display using glass vessels.

PESTS & DISEASES

How can I protect my plants from pests and diseases?

Do you sometimes fear that there's something nasty lurking among your indoor plants, waiting to pounce and suck the life out of your green babies while you're not looking? Well, you're not alone – we can all be planto-chondriacs when it comes to our beloved plant pets! However, there's no need to panic. Even though it's inevitable that at some stage a pest or disease will affect your plants, there are ways and means of dealing with all of them, which I'm going to share with you.

I have a lot of plants and I am always dealing with a pest or disease on this plant or that. The good news is that spotting them early and treating them properly usually results in minimal damage and your plant should recover perfectly. It's vital to identify and treat pests and diseases as soon as possible, as the longer they have free rein, the worse the infestation will become.

The pests and diseases that attack indoor plants come into your home in a variety of ways. Some are tiny and simply blow in on the air through windows and doors, while others hitch a ride on the new plants you bring into your house after a plant-buying expedition. Whatever the case, it's not your fault – it's just a part of growing living things.

What to look for when buying plants

When you are buying a new plant, it's always a good idea to closely inspect it for the telltale signs of insect infestation and fungal infection. Most insect pests like to cluster on the underside of leaves: turn the leaves upside down or lift the pot up, if you're able to, so you can have a good look at them. Wet black or brown spots on leaves can be a sign of fungal infection or damage from cold temperatures. A few yellow leaves are okay, as long as these aren't the only leaves on the plant, but too many is not a good sign. Pass on that plant!

Above all, a new plant should be bright and clear in colour, have firm stems and leaves with a fresh appearance and have very few discoloured or drooping leaves. It's really the same as when you buy fresh veggies: have a think about the reasons why you might choose or reject a head of lettuce or broccoli. It's very much the same set of criteria.

It's important to be realistic, though, because sometimes it doesn't matter if you have an eagle eye for bugs and sick-looking leaves. Tiny eggs or fungal spores that can't be seen without magnification can be present in potting mix or on leaves and can still pop up in the cleanest home. The most important thing is to stay calm and carry on by identifying the problem and treating it promptly.

Observation is key

Prevention is the best cure, so I want you to put on your best Sir David Attenborough voice and quietly observe what's going on with your plants whenever you are interacting with them. We're on the hunt for any pest that might be waiting to suck or munch on the precious sap from our plants, and on alert to spot any fungus that might take advantage of overly wet conditions to spawn and multiply. If you develop a habit of mindfully observing your plants, you will easily handle the ongoing management of your indoor specimens.

Watering is the perfect time to look at the leaves. Pay particular attention to the centre of new growth (the point where the little leaf buds emerge) and to the leaf axils (the part where the stem of the leaf joins the main growing stem or crown of the plant), because insects love to hide in these places. Turn a few leaves upside down, scan the plant for a few moments and if all looks good, move on to the next. If you find something that resembles wildlife or anything that would grow in a Petri dish, it's time to diagnose!

'When you are buying a new plant, it's always a good idea to closely inspect it for the telltale signs of insect infestation and fungal infection.'

Common pests and diseases

How to spot and treat them

So, you've found something a bit suspicious-looking on your plant's leaves, or come across some sick-looking foliage. Here is a rundown of the main culprits when it comes to indoor plant pests and diseases. I'll show you how to spot them and treat them effectively so that your plant will recover and thrive.

TIP:
Always follow the safety directions on the packaging when using sprays to treat your plants. Make sure you use them in a well-ventilated area away from children and pets, and wash your hands well afterwards.

Mealy bugs

One of the most common pests found on indoor plants are mealy bugs, and the great thing about these small insects is the ease of spotting and treating them. They look like small, white, fluffy or waxy balls around 2 mm in size. They can sometimes be seen moving around very slowly and they tend to cluster together into lumps of many insects the more they reproduce and infest a plant. They generally hide in the darker areas of the plant, away from light, and especially on the lower leaves, but they will spread to virtually cover a plant if you don't get rid of them – so once again, don't delay in addressing the problem.

SIGNS OF MEALY BUGS

- Yellowing or yellow blotches on the leaves where the insects are present
- Deformed new growth
- A sticky substance on the leaves or on the surface around the plant's pot
- Visible clusters of insects
- A white powdery substance on the surface around the plant

TREATMENT

If you discover only a few mealy bugs, the easiest treatment is to dip a cotton bud into full-strength methylated spirits and dab this onto each bug. The metho won't harm the plant but will quickly kill the mealy bugs by dehydrating their protective coatings.

If numerous spots on the plant are affected or you can see lots of smaller mealy bugs starting to appear, it's time to spray the entire plant. You can use one of two sprays on these insects, depending on the plant: horticultural white oil spray (see Tip below to make your own) or broad spectrum rose spray.

Both of these sprays work well. Use the rose spray on plants with very thin or delicate leaves and white oil spray on plants with thicker leaves. The oil will add some shine to the leaves and change the patina slightly on velvet-leaved plants, while the rose spray won't. If using the rose spray, follow the directions on the packaging for treatment. If using the white oil, repeat at 10-day intervals until no pests are present.

A plant that has a serious infestation – with large areas covered in mealy bugs and the insects in the soil as well – should be thrown away, pot and all.

TIP:

If you'd like to make your own horticultural white oil, combine 500 ml of vegetable oil with 125 ml of dishwashing detergent in a container and shake well. This base mixture will keep for a couple of months. To use the white oil, add 2 teaspoons to 400 ml of water in a spray bottle. Give it a good shake and you're ready to go.

Spider mites

These tiny relatives of the spider family like to congregate on the underside of leaves and puncture the plant cells to feed, causing damage. They reproduce quickly and soon start to disfigure leaves, weakening the plant and eventually killing it. They are only just visible to the naked eye, but become more noticeable as their numbers increase – they look like tiny moving dots. Spider mites are often accompanied by a very fine web which can be seen when the sun hits the plant from the side. Lightly misting the plant with water will make the webs more visible as well. Mites are fond of hot, dry conditions and are highly active during the warmer months.

TIP:

A magnifying glass is very handy and always in my tool kit when looking for pests. It's a cheap and readily available instrument that allows you to see mites and other plant problems clearly.

SIGNS OF SPIDER MITES

- Tiny white or yellow pinpoint marks on the leaves, especially around the edges, that spread to form a mottled effect
- Leaves that look almost all white or silvery (on plants with heavy infestations)
- Curled leaf edges and distorted new growth
- Leaf drop of infested leaves
- Fine silvery webs covering stems and/or leaves

TIP:

Wet your index fingertip slightly and rub the underside of a leaf you suspect might have spider mites on it. Now rub your fingertip and thumb together – if you feel a gritty sensation like tiny grains of sand, the plant probably has mites.

TREATMENT

If the plant being treated has medium to large leaves, spray the entire plant with water, then gently wipe both sides of the leaves with a soft cloth. This dislodges mites as well as their eggs and webs. Rinse the leaves with water again and let the plant dry before spraying it with one of the treatments below. This step really helps to eradicate the mites but isn't practical for plants with smaller or delicate leaves.

There are a number of different sprays that can be used to treat spider mites:

- Broad spectrum rose spray: this is a chemical spray that is useful against many pests (as well as fungal disease – see page 174). Follow the directions on the packaging.
- Neem oil: a plant-based spray, this is good for treating very light infestations. Spray the plant all over and repeat at 10-day intervals until no pests are present.
- Horticultural soap spray (see Tip below to make your own): this is a non-toxic alternative which is a great treatment for light to moderate infestations. After the initial treatment, spray at 10-day intervals until no pests are present.
- Miticides: these are serious chemicals that need to be applied carefully while wearing protective gear; I steer clear of them for indoor plant application.

TIP:

To make a horticultural soap spray, combine 2 teaspoons of liquid soap and 1 litre of water in a spray bottle. Shake to mix well.

Scale

Scale are small insects that are protected by an almost flat, oval-shaped, waxy shell, which gives them their name. They are 1–2 mm long, depending on the species, and can be pale beige to brown or black in colour; immature scale insects tend to be paler and darken as they mature. Like many other insect pests they suck the sap of plants, causing damage as they do so, and some types produce honeydew, a sticky secretion that attracts ants and encourages fungal disease on the plant. Scale insects will congregate on stems and leaves, and they seem to prefer areas around the veins of the leaves and along stems.

SIGNS OF SCALE

- Small, waxy-looking ovals scattered singly across stems and leaves
- Lumpy or bumpy clusters of oval shells
- A sticky film on leaves and stems
- Yellowing leaves
- Leaf drop

TREATMENT

The best way to kill scale is with horticultural white oil spray (see Tip on page 171 to make your own), which smothers them. Make sure you spray all areas of the plant including the underside of the leaves, and keep the newly sprayed plant out of the sun as the oil magnifies the sun's rays. Some delicate plants, such as ferns and African violets, can be damaged by white oil, so if in doubt spray a small test area first. Plants that are sensitive to white oil can instead be treated with neem oil or horticultural soap (see Tip opposite to make your own), though neem oil is slightly less effective against eggs. After the initial treatment, spray at 10-day intervals until no pests are present. A few days after the first treatment you'll be able to wipe dead scale off your larger leaved plants if you choose.

Aphids

These small insects that suck sap and secrete honeydew aren't too common indoors, but if you notice groups of small crawling insects with six legs and green, black or white bodies clustering around new leaves and growing tips, these will be aphids.

SIGNS OF APHIDS

- Distorted leaves
- Leaf drop
- Sticky leaves

TREATMENT

Aphids are easy to treat – start by washing the insects off the plant with a stream of water. Dislodge as many as you can and then spray with the recommended dilution of neem oil or horticultural soap (see Tip opposite to make your own) to kill any that remain.

Fungal disease

As well as pests there are a number of diseases that can affect our house plants, with the most common being fungal: of these, powdery mildew, leaf spot and rust are the ones that occur most frequently. As they like moist, damp conditions, avoid wetting leaves when they won't have the opportunity to dry quickly, such as in the evenings, especially during the cooler months. Good watering practices can discourage fungus, while overwatering can be another contributor to fungal growth.

SIGNS OF FUNGAL DISEASE

- Black spots on leaves
- Yellow patches on leaves
- Rust-coloured patches or spots on the top or underside of leaves
- Moist or wilting areas within a leaf, stem or crown of a plant
- A mildew-like, powdery coating that is either whiteish or black in colour

TREATMENT

Whichever fungus is affecting your plants, numerous anti-fungal sprays or fungicides are available, ranging from organic to broad spectrum systemic varieties. I have used many different types and almost all have been effective against most kinds of fungus. To treat, spray all of the plant well, including the stems and the underside of leaves.

Root and crown rot

Rot is another manifestation of fungus, and it is one of the most devastating things that can happen to a plant – it will very quickly kill it by destroying the root system or literally cutting the plant off at soil level by rotting its main stems. Overwatering is the biggest contributing factor to the development of rot.

SIGNS OF ROT

- Plant wilting even when watered properly
- Slow to no growth
- Plant falling over in the pot
- Many leaves yellowing and dropping
- Upon inspection, roots appear mushy and soft

TREATMENT

It isn't always possible to save a plant suffering from rot, but the earlier you detect the fungus the better the chances. Take the plant out of its pot and gently remove as much of the dead and rotten roots and stem as possible. Dispose of as much old soil as you can. If the roots or crown are completely gone you'll have no option but to dispose of the plant.

If some healthy roots and a good portion of the stem remain, you might be able to save the plant. Wash any remaining soil from the healthy leaves and spray the entire root ball and stem of the plant with an anti-fungal spray. Take a new pot or wash the old one in dishwashing detergent or a bleach solution and pot up the plant patient using fresh soil. Spray the leaves and stems with more fungicide, but don't water the plant yet. Let it sit for a couple of days and then water it moderately. Keep the soil barely moist and wait – new growth and the stems and leaves perking up will be a good sign that your plant is recovering, at which point you can resume normal watering.

Fungus gnats

Ever had a tiny fly-like insect about 3 mm long try to fly up your nose when you're looking at a plant? It's likely to be a fungus gnat, and they are truly annoying as they seem to be attracted to people's faces – but relax, they don't bite. They love moist, warm soil and are encouraged to breed by constant moisture, so check your watering regimen to make sure you're not overdoing it. These pests don't do a lot of damage but in large numbers they reduce a plant's growth rate because the larvae in the soil will eat the roots. I get a lot of questions about how to eradicate fungus gnats. It's not difficult, just follow the directions below.

SIGNS OF FUNGUS GNATS

- Small, whiteish larvae crawling in the soil
- Slow growth and wilting (on advanced infestations)
- Small, fly-like insects around plants and pots

TREATMENT

A solution of peroxide and water is my go-to for stamping out gnats. Mix 1 part 3 per cent peroxide (available from chemists) with 4 parts water and use it to water the soil of affected plants well. The solution will fizz a bit, and this is normal – it kills the larvae on contact but is harmless to plants.

Another sure-fire treatment is to use food-grade diatomaceous earth (available online and at pet shops), which is a fine powder made of the tiny shells of fossilised organisms known as diatoms. The powder doesn't harm plants but acts like shredded glass on the larvae of fungus gnats. It needs to be food grade as this is safe and non-toxic, but as with any product containing dust, be sure to use it in a well-ventilated area. Diatomaceous earth has to be applied to a dry surface so it's best to treat a plant a day or so after it was last watered. Then it's a matter of simply sprinkling it on the top of the potting mix like icing sugar. A small amount goes a long way: I use around 1 heaped teaspoon for an 18 cm nursery pot.

TIP:

If you're not sure which pot the fungus gnats flying around your house are coming from, put a small piece of potato on top of the mix in the pot you suspect may be harbouring them. It will attract the gnat's larvae out of the soil and then you will know which plant to treat.

‘If you develop a habit of mindfully observing your plants, you will easily handle the ongoing management of your indoor specimens.’

STYLING & DESIGNING

Plants as the ultimate indoor art

When it comes to indoor plants, my motto is that any surface is a plant shelf and any container a pot! If you follow my Instagram account @craigmilran you'll already know about my penchant for styling up a leaf storm in every room of my home. I firmly believe that plants can be the ultimate indoor art – Christies and Sotheby's might not agree, but who needs expensive art on the walls when you can have stunning, sculptural plants in pots, growing and responding every day to your care?

Along with indulging my plant passion, I have been designing furniture and homewares for more than 25 years as part of MRD home, a business I started while working in a plant nursery. It has never occurred to me that my indoor plants shouldn't be a part of my interior design ethos or that they can't be as powerful and inspiring as a stunning piece of furniture or light fitting in an interior scheme.

Styling your home with plants isn't exactly a new idea. The Chinese were using them as interior accents around 1000 BCE, and between 500 and 400 BCE the ancient civilisations of Rome, Egypt and Greece brought the outdoors inside as well, with wealthier citizens using house plants as status symbols. In the fifteenth century and onwards, as the idea of using plants to bring life and beauty indoors spread across Europe and exotic plants became objects of desire, a single plant could fetch the equivalent of tens of thousands of dollars.

For me, interiors and living plants have always gone hand in hand, and it's with great joy, a sense of amazement and maybe a little incredulity that I find myself in the middle of a fabulous resurgence of decorating with plants in the home. Over the years I have not only developed many techniques for incorporating plants into rooms and spaces, but also for designing my plant specimens themselves. Just as outdoor gardeners prune, shape and manicure trees and shrubs into unique and complementary forms, I've searched for ways to grow and display my plant pals to deliver extra oomph and a sense of the unexpected, treating them more like sculptures than pot plants. (See page 209 for more information on pruning, training and maintenance.)

In this chapter we're going to have so much fun elevating our house plants and accessorising them to the next level, creating gorgeous indoor vistas and yes, some Insta-worthy moments that are sure to get lots of oohs and aahs from friends, family and followers alike.

Styling basics

The laws of plant chemistry

By following certain natural laws of styling and arranging objects, we can create vignettes that are pleasing to the eye. These rules are universal and they apply equally to our indoor plants; once you learn them, you will be amazed at how your indoor plants sing as a part of your interior. Designing and displaying your plant collection will bring you a new appreciation of your plant family, so follow me on the road to plant-styling perfection.

Any container is a pot

Oh, how I love this one! This is my excuse for buying almost any vessel that takes my fancy and including it in my styling arsenal of pots and planters. Seriously, there are so many beautiful bowls, vases, glasses, baskets, jugs and jars to collect, and there *will* be a plant that will sit perfectly in nearly every one. 'But the opening is too small for a plant,' I hear you say. Tell that to the mini air plant (*Tillandsia ionantha*) that sits ever so perfectly on top!

This is one of the main reasons why I grow all of my plants in plastic nursery pots, which I like to think of as underwear for plants. The fun comes when you dress up your plants – you can change their outer, decorative pots whenever you like. Remember, a cheap plastic pot can be easily cut down with a pair of scissors to fit a shallower container, and plants can be placed on top of upturned plastic saucers or containers to lift them to the perfect height in deeper vessels.

Any piece that isn't water resistant – such as a woven rope basket, felt laundry bin or wooden bowl, for example – only needs a plastic saucer placed in the base. Use rigid, deep-profile saucers as they are less likely to spill when you lift them out. They also act as a solid base for fabric and woven holders, helping them to hold their shape. Keep your eyes open for interesting containers and you will soon be amazed at how many options exist to accessorise and raise your plants to the next level.

Don't be too serious: mix your greens

Don't worry too much about creating displays that have the correct level of bright light for each plant, unless you want them to stay put in one position for a long period of time (for more information, see the Light and Location chapter on page 109). Personally, I find it great fun to create 'moments' with my plants on coffee or console tables, sideboards, podiums, bedside tables, window ledges or, for larger pots, the floor. I mix plant types like hairy white cacti with variegated tropicals or sculptural succulents with flowering orchids, focusing more on how the shapes, colours and textures work together than their individual care requirements.

Most plants will tolerate low light for 2–3 weeks and some much longer, so as soon as you get tired of the display or a plant starts to tell you it needs more light because it's leaning towards the window, move it to a brighter position. Don't be afraid to mix fresh cut flowers, leaves or cuttings in vases with potted plants for a fresh take on botanical design – they go together beautifully and, again, it's a bit unexpected so carries more design weight. The whole point is to stop you, and anyone else in your home, in your tracks, making you do a double take, admiring the perfect beauty of nature every time you walk past or glance over.

Odd numbers

It's a fact – odd numbers look better in most settings, and plants are no exception. That's because a slightly off-balance, asymmetrical arrangement keeps our brain interested in each of the individual elements in the group and forces our eye to take in not only the vignette but the room around it. Perfect symmetry appears unnatural and forced, especially in relation to styling indoor plants.

One or the other principle

This is my plant version of Coco Chanel's famous quote, 'Before you leave the house, look in the mirror and take one thing off.' When choosing a plant for a pot, only one of them should be the star: a simple pale planter begs for a showy, patterned plant and, vice versa, if you have a colourful or unique patterned pot, pare the look back with a simple plant of uniform colour. This approach also works well when combining plants for a vignette. For example, if I'm choosing three plants to sit together, I usually combine three different leaf types: I'll select a plant with a large, simple, flat leaf, like a philodendron; a plant that has a smaller leaf that's a bit more detailed, such as a mini monstera (*Rhaphidophora tetrasperma*); and a plant that has a patterned leaf, like a prayer plant or a variegated specimen. This is because three different plants that all have bold patterns or complex leaf forms would be hectic and not the calm effect that I want to create. However, if you happen to love clashing patterns and colours, then go ahead, I support you – it's just not my style.

Pots first, plants second

Always follow this rule if you want a cohesive, striking result. This method is especially good when you are just starting to introduce plants to a particular area in your home or when you decide it's time for a rearrange and refresh of your existing plantscapes. If you imagine a decorative planter as being like a piece of furniture that needs to tie in with the other elements in a room, then just like any other item you'd add to your interior, it makes sense to ensure that it looks perfect next to your sofa or on the coffee table first, before you decide what plant to put in it. Many people do this the other way around: they buy a plant for a particular spot and then find a pot to go with it … and then they do this again and again. The result tends to be less than perfect and a bit haphazard – instead, choose the pot and its location first, and then choose a plant that suits the pot and, ideally, the light in that position.

Triangles

This is a well-known principle of display that has been used for centuries, and it's something to which I gravitated towards naturally before knowing it was even a thing. Imagining a triangle and then placing objects within its borders creates arrangements that are balanced and aesthetically pleasing. The principle can be used to organise anything from tiny tabletop groupings to massive installations of potted trees with equal success.

'When it comes to indoor plants, my motto is that any surface is a plant shelf and any container a pot!'

Suspended plants

The fourth plant dimension

There are many areas in our homes where we can display plants that are usually off our radar because they seem impractical or difficult. However, I'm here to tell you that with a few simple tricks you can incorporate living art on your walls and utilise vertical space in your home by suspending plants from walls and ceilings. The very fact that these spaces are often ignored adds to the impact when they are used because the result is unexpected and fascinating. You don't need to install large hanging baskets either, even though these can look amazing if you have the space and easy access to water them. Instead, you can make an elegant display of smaller plants above a bedside table or on a bare wall that needs some texture and interest. In fact, when creating a display using the triangle principle described on page 187, think about using a hanging plant as the apex for real wow factor.

If you are able to drill into your walls and ceilings to fix permanent hooks, then of course you have a lot of options in regard to the size and weight of the plants you'll be able to hang, and you can let your imagination run wild. Even if you're not able to do this, there are still many solutions and ideas for suspending plants. The first thing you need to consider before you hang any plant is the potting mix – you want to use a potting mix that's lighter in weight than standard mix for ease of handling and safety (see page 95 for how to make my light mix, which is perfect for the job). Once that's taken care of, here are some of my tips for hanging plants in the home.

Removable adhesive hooks

Removable hooks are a great way to hang planters from walls or smaller, lighter plants from the ceiling without damaging the surface – brilliant if you're renting! I use clear, self-adhesive wall hooks, with a movable metal hook, to suspend plants that weigh up to about 4 kg. The hooks I use can actually support up to 8 kg, but I halve it to be on the safe side, particularly if I'm going to attach it to the ceiling. Weigh the plant and its pot on your kitchen scales if you're not sure of the weight; most smaller plants in 10 cm or 12 cm pots come in anywhere from 600 g to 1.5 kg. You don't have to weigh the plant straight after watering it, but it pays to keep in mind how much this will add to the weight – so perhaps pop it on the scale a few hours after giving it a drink. You can opt for lighter weight hanging pots or make your own using decorative plastic pots (see How to make a plant wall, page 196). When using removable hooks, my light potting mix (see page 95) comes in handy – by reducing the weight of the soil, you can have more plant!

Tension rods

Tension rods are no-drill, spring-loaded rods that fit between two vertical surfaces and hold up to 11 kg, depending on their size and construction. They're available in lengths that range from 60 cm to 3 m. Tension rods are ideal for suspending plants in windows, skylights, nooks and even wide doorways in open-plan living areas. As always, check the weight of the plants you're hanging so you don't overload the rods.

Retractable plant pulleys

Pulleys are a great and affordable idea that allow you to raise and lower your hanging plants to water and maintain them without the bother or risk of climbing on a stool or ladder. They also give you the ability to position a plant or group of plants at the perfect height for display, because you can choose where to stop as you move them up or down. They come in sizes that will support up to 15 kg and are a must if you want to make your hanging gardens of Babylon fuss free.

'Don't be afraid to mix fresh or dried flowers, leaves or cuttings in vases with potted plants for a fresh take on botanical design – they go together beautifully and it's a bit unexpected so carries more design weight.'

How to

MAKE A PLANT WALL

A few years back I had a big blank wall in my home and decided to make a plant wall with a difference. I wanted the pots to be a sculptural element in the overall effect – so rather than have a wall full of plants overgrowing each other, I wanted to create a wall of strategically placed specimens, like an art installation. It's still one of the most commented-on features in my home and it's so easy to recreate, even for people who are renting and aren't able to drill into the walls; the steps below outline a damage-free, removable option as well as a version that uses shelf brackets. This project creates a plant wall of six hanging plants but the number can of course be adjusted to as many as you wish to hang on your wall.

YOU WILL NEED:

- Pencil and paper
- 6 white-painted L-shaped 150 × 125 mm shelf brackets with 12 screws to fit *or* 6 heavy-duty adhesive wall hooks with transparent backs
- 12 plaster mates (if affixing brackets to plasterboard walls)
- Power drill
- 6 lightweight decorative 14 cm polypropylene (PP) pots with no drainage holes (14 cm is ideal for the bracket size specified, and ensures your plant is a workable weight for removable hooks)
- Clear high-strength fishing line (16 kg break point and above)
- 6 small plastic saucers that fit inside the bottom of the pots
- 6 potted plants

1

2

3

4

5

6

7

1 Start by visualising where you want the plants to sit on the wall; it really helps to do a sketch and decide in advance. Draw in where the brackets or hooks will sit as well as a rough outline of where each plant will hang. Asymmetry looks best, with some pots higher and others lower, and when you look at the wall from a distance the plants should all have roughly the same amount of empty space around them for a balanced look. Mix trailing plants with clumping species for visual interest and allow for trailing stems when positioning the pots.

2 Now mark on the wall with a pencil where you need to affix each bracket or hook. Secure each bracket or hook to the wall (follow the directions provided on the packaging for the latter).

3 Next make three evenly spaced marks around the perimeter of each decorative pot with a pencil, each about 1 cm below the top edge. Visualise a triangle on the top of the pot to assist in positioning the holes: you will have a hole at each point of the triangle. Carefully drill the three holes through each planter. Keep them as small as possible, though large enough for you to thread the fishing line through.

4 Now cut three lengths of fishing line for each pot to the length you want each plant to hang, adding another 20 cm to each to allow for tying off at both ends.

5 Take a pot, thread a piece of fishing line through each hole and double-knot its end. Carry the pot to the wall. If you're hanging the pot from a bracket, hold the three pieces of fishing line together above the pot at the length you want it to hang, and thread the lines through the hole at the end of the bracket, making sure the top of the pot is level. Tie the lines together in a double-knot above the bracket to fasten, then cut off any stray ends to tidy things up.

If you're using removable hooks, hold the three pieces of fishing line together above the pot at the level of the hook, making sure the pot is sitting against the wall at the length you want it to hang. The top of the pot will be on an angle: to level it out, pull the fishing line closest to the wall up so that it is shorter than the line furthest from the wall. Tie the lengths into a double knot, trim off any stray ends and hang the pot on the hook. Repeat for each of the decorative pots.

6 Put a small plastic saucer upside down in the bottom of each pot.

7 Now your hanging holders are ready to accessorise with their plant partners. Have fun playing with different combinations of plants.

DIY designer planters

Creating my own designer planters is my favourite styling hack for an instant collection of top-end, stylish vessels for a low-end price.

Colour me happy

I often find beautifully shaped, affordable decorative planters in the wrong colours. For example, if you have a quick wander through your local nursery's planter section it will yield lots of pots that look amazing together shape-wise but really clash in colour and finish. The solution is to paint them! Matte spray paint is available in a huge range of colours; I mostly go for neutral shades such as white, ivory, black and grey but I've also used pale aqua, olive green and terracotta to great effect. You can spray-paint nearly every surface except shiny glass and plastic because you'll find the paint peels off. However, even some textured gloss surfaces hold paint well. For an uber stylish look, use chalkboard paint – I love the uneven surface it creates, and the super matte finish gives the pieces a real high-fashion look. This type of paint comes in a range of colours, it adheres well to most surfaces and it's quite economical for large planters.

TIP:

Painting decorative planters is a great way to update pots that you already own but that no longer fit with your colour scheme.

DIY podium planter

Another great hack is to glue different pots together to create on-trend podium-type planters. Choose two pots and flip one upside down to act as the base, then sit the other one on top and see how it looks. Have a play with lots of combinations before you buy – mix up proportions until you find the pots and sizes that are just right. Fasten them together with a strong construction-type adhesive, available from any hardware store, and let it set before you use them. There is so much potential to be creative here. My DIY podium planters opposite are all white, but you could paint the base one shade of green, for example, and the top a different shade of green for a totally fashionable look for a fraction of the price you would pay for a designer pot. This makes for a fun (supervised!) afternoon for the kids, too, and is a great way of getting them inspired and interested in plants.

Clear glass vases and temporary terrariums

I love the idea of plants in glass but I'm not a big fan of bottle-type terrariums packed with plants, even though they can look great in photos. Maybe it's because you can buy them almost everywhere now and they seem a little 'busy' to me; plus they require a lot of maintenance to keep them looking good, as they tend to get overgrown fairly quickly.

My take on terrariums is to place one or two small potted plants inside simple, clear glass vases for maximum effect. You don't even need to disguise the pots if the colours match and they're simple in form, but you can also pack sphagnum moss, pebbles, coir fibre or orchid bark around the pots to cover them and provide a contrasting base to your display. Any vessel suits this concept as long as the opening is large enough to get a plant through and to allow you to water them when they need it. Temporary terrariums look spectacular in groups of three or more as table centrepieces.

The added advantage of these glass vessels is that they create a microclimate around the plants, and if you keep the substrate around the pots moist they become the perfect mini greenhouse environment for smaller, tropical species that thrive in higher humidity. This includes plants like nerve plant (*Fittonia*), prayer plants, jewel orchids (*Ludisia*, *Macodes*), club moss (*Selaginella*), Venus flytrap (*Dionaea muscipula*), pitcher plant (*Nepenthes*), air plant (*Tillandsia ionantha*), small ferns and peperomias, to name a few. You can also create a chic, arid version with a minimalist vibe by using cacti or succulents, and instead of moss or bark, use coarse sand or pebbles to finish the look.

TIP:

When handling cacti, use rolled-up newspaper to create a holder that keeps the spines away from your fingers. Roll the paper into a tube and then flatten it like tape. Wrap it around the middle of the cacti and hold the two ends together so you are gripping the plant firmly. Voila! You can lift it without getting stabbed.

‘If you have a quick wander through your local nursery’s planter section, it will yield lots of pots that look amazing together shape-wise but really clash in colour and finish. The solution is to paint them!’

5 Litres

Plant stands

Elevate to fascinate! Lifting a plant off the floor, whether by placing it on a simple podium or on a stand, has the visual effect of isolating it from its surroundings, giving it a sense of grandeur and importance. I love to move my favourite plant of the week into the spotlight, so to speak, by putting it on a podium in my kitchen/dining room, where I can admire it and appreciate its uniqueness. When placing plants in a group, a pot stand provides height that can highlight a smaller plant that would otherwise get lost among larger ones. Pot stands are also a great idea when you want to put a plant next to a sofa or occasional chair – or anywhere with limited space, for that matter – but there isn't room for a side table. There are lots of stands on the market now constructed from timber or metal, and there's sure to be some that match your style. For added interest, choose two or three of different heights and arrange them with the tallest at the back, medium to the side and lowest to the front.

Plant shelves

The plant shelfie even has its own hashtag, and for good reason. Shelves are a fabulous way to display a collection of plants and planters that keeps the 'tapestry of leaves' to one area of a space. I like to call this 'enclosed chaos': the real bonus of a plant shelf is that it enables you to incorporate lots of plants into an interior scheme while maintaining a sense of calm and intention. To illustrate the opposite of this effect, and why a shelf works so well, imagine all the plants housed on that shelf placed randomly on various surfaces across a room ... that is chaos not so enclosed!

As your plant collection grows or if you want to keep your plants to one area, shelves are the go-to solution, and there are so many options to choose from. I'm a fan of asymmetrically set, floating shelves placed at different heights and loaded with a selection of both trailers and clumping plant types to make the most of the vertical and horizontal spaces – for example, I might use jungle cacti (*Rhipsalis*, *Epiphyllum*) and wax plant (*Hoya*) for trailing interest, and peperomias and arrowhead plant (*Syngonium*) for height. Floating shelves are readily available, affordable and come in a range of colours and timber finishes to suit all interiors.

There's no need to stop at simple shelves, though: I once painted an old second-hand cabinet with white paint inside and out, tied the doors wide open (I could also have opted to remove the doors) and filled the inner shelves with plants spilling over the edges. The effect of all of this living, green texture enclosed within a chic cupboard was striking. I often eye that black-coated, metal mesh, industrial shelving at my local hardware store and think how cool this would be for a plantastic display solution if I lived in a vintage home or industrial-style space. With shelves there's so much on offer – the only limit is your imagination. Remember, 'any surface is a plant shelf'... who said that again? Lol.

‘My take on terrariums is to place one or two small potted plants inside simple, clear glass vases for maximum effect.’

MAINTENANCE, GROOMING & TRAINING

How to keep your plants looking their best

Now that you're using the correct potting mixes, have your pest-free plants placed in the spots that suit them perfectly and they are looking spectacular in their designer pots, it's time to talk maintenance. Plants are continually growing and changing, a bit like our hair. Buying a perfect plant, not maintaining it and getting frustrated that it's looking unruly is like getting a great haircut and wondering why, six months later, it doesn't look so good!

One thing I can guarantee you is that no plant is going to look the same a year after you bought it. Hopefully it will have grown fuller and larger, which is what we all want, after all, but there comes a point in any plant's life when it needs a haircut, or maybe something more severe like a heavy prune – or even a total makeover. Eventually most plants get leggy, either too tall or too long, they lose leaves, creating unsightly bare patches, and some don't do as well as we would like and need to be cut back to stumps or restarted from cuttings. Maintenance is the key and the tips in this chapter will ensure your potted friends stay well groomed and glowing with vitality.

Plants that climb or spread outwards as they grow will need support and training to help them look their very best. We will cover how to use stakes, trellises and totems to not only control how much space a plant uses and to keep it neat and tidy, but also to give it its best life. Many plants that climb, for example, will do far better when attached to a support of one kind or another.

Day-to-day maintenance

Whenever I walk around the house or water my plants I keep an eye out for yellow leaves, spent flowers and brown leaf edges, and I make a mental note to revisit the plants that need some TLC when I next have some free time. If you have only a few plants, once a month is enough to check them and do some finessing to keep them in tiptop form. The larger your collection, the more frequently you should check – at least every couple of weeks to make sure you're not missing anything. Dead and dying leaves are places pests such as mealy bugs and scale insects like to hide, so remove them from the plant and, if they've fallen, from the soil and area around the plant. Yellowing and dropping of old leaves is a completely normal phenomenon and shouldn't be cause for alarm unless it's accompanied by any pests and diseases or if it's happening a lot to the same plant.

Pruning and trimming

To keep your plants looking neat and well cared for, at some point it will be necessary to cut their leaves and stems. 'Cut my plants?!' I hear you gasp … the answer is a definite yes, and once you get used to pruning and trimming plants it becomes second nature and much easier to do. Many house plants grow quite quickly and start to sprawl outwards, while some have a naturally untidy growth habit. Others may look fine but become too large or trail too long for the spot you want to keep them in. The answer is to strategically remove some of the plant.

It's a great idea to have a dedicated plant ICU or rehab shelf – somewhere in your home that's out of the way but still gets good light – to put plants that have had major cosmetic work done on them. This way they can recover to their full glory before you return them to the spotlight in the main living areas.

Pruning in spring or summer is ideal so that the plant can rejuvenate itself as quickly as possible; you also don't want to encourage delicate new growth in cooler months because it could be damaged by cold temperatures. It takes a bit of practice to feel confident with pruning plants back hard and it's completely normal to feel nervous at first – start with a plant that's not one of your expensive favourites. Once you have seen a plant bounce back better than it was before after a good prune you will feel more confident to do the chop on others.

TIP:

Make sure you prune your plants with sharp scissors or secateurs – a blunt blade can damage stems and leave your plants vulnerable to disease. As a general rule, cut stems on an angle to prevent water from sitting on the cut and causing rot.

How much should I prune off my plants?

Is it going to be a full cut-astrophe, or just a trim? To answer this question, we need to look at how you want the plant to look, the type of plant and the growing conditions.

Fast-growing plants that have become 'leggy' and unattractive with bare lower stems will need a hard prune: cut these back to around 10–20 cm above the soil line. They will look even uglier for a while, but once they start sprouting they will soon take on a compact and bushy appearance again.

TIP:

When pruning, it's good practice to cut a centimetre or so above a leaf node. This enables the new growth to sprout freely and avoids leaving too much stem to die back above the node.

Plants that have reached a size you are happy with and which you don't want to grow much larger can be kept in check by tying in or pruning off stray branches. Trailing plants that have grown too long respond well to having the ends snipped off – when you do this, think about how you want the plant to look in 6 to 12 months. You need to allow for future growth when you trim because if you cut the ends to where you want them now, in a few months' time they will reshoot and before you know it the plant will be too long once more.

Certain indoor plants – such as alocasias, prayer plants (*Ctenanthe*, *Goeppertia*, *Maranta*, *Stromanthe*), fiddle-leaf fig (*Ficus lyrata*) and variegated plants – are prone to developing brown edges and leaf tips, and this can be a normal part of leaf ageing, or senescence. I receive a lot of questions relating to this, and most people assume that their humidity is too low or water quality is at fault. It's certainly possible that very dry air can cause brown edges on delicate leaves, but if you have ever seen tropical plants growing in their native jungle habitats you will notice that there are brown leaves and edges on those plants, too! In fact, wild specimens can look very untidy and quite different to the perfectly groomed plants we buy in nurseries. Variegated plants with delicate white areas that tend to brown at the drop of a hat also need more trips to the salon (aka my kitchen bench).

Trimming the brown edges from leaves works wonders to freshen up these plants. Use a sharp pair of scissors and carefully trim the brown off the leaf, keeping as much healthy leaf as possible and making sure you retain the natural shape so the trimmed leaves don't stand out too much. You may find the browning creeps back onto the leaf again; if this happens, just trim it off again.

TIP:

Remember to wipe your scissors clean with methylated spirits in between plants to ensure you don't spread any diseases from plant to plant.

‘Use a sharp pair of scissors and carefully trim the brown off the leaf, keeping as much healthy leaf as possible and making sure you retain the natural shape so the trimmed leaves don’t stand out too much.’

Shaping your plants

Are the leaves of your plants not doing what you want them to? It's time for an obedience lesson! I keep a reel of plastic-coated wire garden tie in my kitchen draw. It's something I use almost every day to keep unruly stems in place and to shift leaves to sit where I want them to on plants. If you've never done this before, let's take a look at how to go about it.

If you have a plant such as an arrowhead plant (*Syngonium*) whose stems are spreading outwards and starting to flop over, take a length of tie and, end in each hand, loop it around the plant about halfway up the stems. Tighten it gently so that it pulls them inwards until you like how the plant is looking, and simply tie the ends together. If it's a large plant, put a bamboo stake in one side of the pot, hide it among the leaves and fasten the tie to it for extra support.

For climbing plants that need a support, put a stake behind the main stem(s) of the plant and use it as a framework for tying up individual stems – however, by far my favourite support and training method for climbers is a round totem or a flat panel filled with sphagnum moss or coir peat (see page 226 for step-by-step instructions on how to make a totem).

Leaf training

Larger plants with fewer leaves like Swiss cheese plant (*Monstera deliciosa*), philodendrons and palms, for example, depend on even spacing and positioning of the leaves for balance and visual appeal. One missing leaf or another leaning off in the wrong direction can really detract from what would be an otherwise perfect display plant! It can also make the plant look messy and untidy, which is not the @craigmilran way (I have been known to get fairly mad with myself if I accidentally break off a crucial leaf or if a leaf that is the focal point develops a spot or blemish). Now, you might not be as obsessed as me, but a bit of leaf training can be fun and also give you stunning specimens that will leave you with a huge sense of satisfaction. And the good news is that even if you do accidentally damage a star leaf you can manoeuvre things so the plant gets its balance back.

Whenever you want to bend stems or leaves, it's always best to do it when the plant is thirsty rather than freshly watered. This way the stems are softer and more pliable – the last thing I want is for you to hear the 'snap' that plant lovers dread. Before you begin, take a good look at the plant: is there a leaf that looks out of place, or are there too many leaves on one side and not enough on the other? If you decide only a leaf or two needs to be moved slightly, fasten some tie around a leaf on the side of the plant directly opposite the leaf you want to move, and then pass the tie gently through the plant, looping it around the errant leaf. Make the tie short enough so that it gently pulls the leaf to where you want it to sit; a little twist will fasten the end and you can trim off the excess with scissors. You can do this over and again on the same plant until it takes on the form you want, and the tie will be mostly hidden behind the leaves and stems. After 2–3 weeks the stems will have set and you can remove the ties.

For larger plants with sturdy stems like Swiss cheese plant (*Monstera deliciosa*), you may need to use a strong stake – push it into the pot in a position that enables you to tie a leaf or two in the direction you want. Remember, a few weeks is all that's needed before you can remove the stake and the leaf will stay in its new position.

‘I keep a reel of plastic-coated wire garden tie in my kitchen drawer. It’s something I use almost every day to keep unruly stems in place and to shift leaves to sit where I want them to on plants.’

Supports for your plants

Many popular indoor plants are climbers or tall growers that need support to keep heavy stems from leaning over and possibly breaking. Climbing plants, especially pothos (*Epipremnum aureum*), Swiss cheese plant (*Monstera deliciosa*) and various philodendrons, will respond to physical support by producing larger leaves. Growing a plant on a stake, trellis or totem tricks the plant into thinking it's growing on a tree – any roots growing from the main stem (aerial roots) will fasten onto the support. Just watch how large the leaves grow then! Totems in particular look very striking and are a perfect way to keep these kinds of plants tidy and controlled in an interior setting.

Stakes

Any plant that is getting tall and unstable will benefit from a stake to support it. For plants like cane-stemmed begonias, a couple of slender stakes will be all that's needed: simply insert them into the mix a few centimetres from the base of the plant and tie the canes to the stakes at various points with garden twine or plastic-coated wire tie. Some plants become top heavy the larger they get – alocasias are a good example of this – and these plants need stakes to keep them from toppling over. Use green-coated metal stakes for medium to larger plants and green or black wooden ones for smaller pots, and they'll be virtually invisible when nestled among the leaves and stems. Insert them a few centimetres from the base of the plant on the opposite side to the one they are leaning to. Ensure that they are firm, and then fasten the base of the plant to the stake to hold the plant upright. Soft rubber or Velcro garden ties are great for securing larger stems; the finer plastic-coated wire ties can cut into large, heavy stems.

Trellises

Vining climbers look amazing sprawling over surfaces or tumbling over shelves, but if you prefer to contain them, a trellis is a good alternative. Plants like rex begonia vine (*Cissus discolor*), Celebes pepper (*Piper ornatum*) and English ivy (*Hedera helix*) all love to meander over trellises. I adore browsing the range of trellises at my local hardware store. The vegetable trellises are especially good because they tend to be simple, minimalist shapes that let the plant be the star. When you first introduce a trellis, tie the stems onto it using some soft garden tie – this helps the plant to attach and also means you can balance the distribution of the stems from the start.

Totems

Some of the most popular indoor plants in Australia and around the globe are climbing aroids. These plants twine their way up trees towards the jungle canopy to reach the light, and they have evolved to grow larger stems and leaves as they increase in height. Many aroids are grown as trailing plants: specimens such as pothos (*Epipremnum aureum*) and Swiss cheese vine (*Monstera adansonii*) look fabulous tumbling out of baskets and pots when they have smaller leaves. However, if you want to create larger, upright specimens, totemise to maximise is the motto *de jour*. You will achieve much larger, mature leaves on many of these plants if you grow them on a support. It's also a very sculptural, tamed result, which suits modern interiors to a T.

‘Growing a plant on a stake, trellis or totem tricks the plant into thinking it’s growing on a tree – any roots growing from the main stem will fasten onto the support. Just watch how large the leaves grow then!’

How to

MAKE YOUR OWN TOTEM

You can buy pre-made totems constructed from just coir fibre from most nurseries and garden stores, and while these are great in some ways, they don't hold moisture very well. I prefer to make my own, using sustainably sourced sphagnum moss. I have also experimented with other materials to create moisture-retaining totems and have found premium grade coir mulch to be an excellent and economical alternative. Instead of only long, fine coir fibres, as found in coir peat, coir mulch is a mix of different-sized coconut material that absorbs rather than repels water.

The average totem requires a 23 cm strip of mesh to give you a finished totem with a 7 cm diameter, the perfect size for most plants. The height of the totem is up to you; the width of the mesh rolls is generally around 90 cm, which means that if you cut a piece 23 cm × 90 cm long, it will roll into a totem that's 90 cm tall. I plant my totems right at the bottom of the pot for stability, so allow for this when you're thinking about the height you need for your totem.

YOU WILL NEED:

- Coir mulch or sphagnum moss
- Plastic bucket
- Plastic-coated wire garden mesh, preferably with a 12 mm grid, and about 90 cm wide
- Plastic-coated wire garden tie
- Large scissors or wire cutters
- Plastic nursery pot, large enough to accommodate the base of the totem and the root ball of the plant
- Appropriate potting mix (see Soil, Pots and Repotting chapter, page 79)
- Plant that requires a totem
- Soft ties (optional)

1
2
3
4
5
6
7
8

1 Place the coir mulch or moss in a bucket and moisten it with enough water that it clumps together.

2 Take your plastic-coated wire garden mesh and cut it into a 23 cm x 90 cm piece. Bend it into a cylinder shape, keeping it open along the long edge so you can pack it with filler.

3 Pick up a handful of coir mulch or moss and squeeze out any excess water to create a wad as big as your fist. Pack it into one end of the rolled mesh, and repeat this step until you have filled about 15–20 cm of the cylinder.

4 Cut a length of wire tie approximately 20 cm long and thread it through the two open edges of the mesh at the end of the cylinder. Pull the two edges together and twist to tie it off, then trim the loose ends and repeat the tying process approximately 15 cm higher, roughly at the point up to which you have packed the mulch or moss. Repeat steps 3 and 4 until you have packed the entire totem, with ties evenly spaced along the join.

5 Congratulations – you have now made a totem, and your plants are going to love you for it! Now it's time to attach the plant to your totem. It's helpful to pot up a totem plant on a kitchen bench or a table where you can rest the totem against a wall to keep it in place. Put the totem into the pot with the base of the totem sitting on the bottom of the pot and the back of the totem against the back of the pot. Pour in some potting mix to stabilise the totem.

6 Take your plant and sit it in front of the totem at the level you want it. Tie it gently to the totem using some soft tie or wire garden tie.

7 Fill in around the roots and totem as you would when potting normally, knocking the pot a few times on the bench to settle the mix. Make sure there is enough mix around the totem to keep it firm within the pot, and keep filling until the mix sits around 3 cm from the top of the pot.

8 Water the plant and totem well and voila! Don't expect it to look perfect straight away, but once the plant starts to climb and the leaves correct themselves and begin to sit nicely, your totemtastic plant will be well on its way. To encourage plants to produce aerial roots that will fasten onto a totem, keep the area behind the stem slightly moist between waterings. You don't need to wet it constantly but when it dries out, give it enough mist to dampen that area – this will help encourage root growth until it's time to water the whole plant and totem again.

TIP:

Some heavy plants or tall totems may need extra support to keep them firmly upright. Take a plastic-coated metal garden stake, place it directly behind the totem and push it into the pot until it hits the bottom. Tie the stake to the totem by threading tie through the mesh and twisting it around the stake to fasten securely.

PROPAGATION

Propagate to populate

What could be more exciting than creating a new plant, at virtually no cost and in the comfort of your own home? I've been fascinated by propagation since my plant journey began all those years ago as a four-year-old. At first I found it hard to believe that some plants – such as rex begonias, for example – can be propagated from a little piece of leaf as small as 2 × 2 cm. As long as there is a leaf vein you can plant it in the correct mix and wait, and sure enough a tiny little plant will start to form. Soon you will have an exact replica of the plant you took the leaf from (what's known as the 'mother plant').

Propagation is the process of making more plants. It's a terrific and fun way to increase your collection for a fraction of the cost of buying plants – and you can keep the new ones to decorate your home, gift them to friends or even sell them to other plant collectors. There are many platforms now where plant hobbyists swap and sell as a way of adding to the enjoyment of their passion for plants. Another great reason to propagate is to create more plants to pot back into the mother plant: this produces a lush, bushier specimen that's lovely to look at.

There are several methods of propagation. Growing from seed is possible but can be complicated for indoor varieties; it also takes a long time for a plant to grow from seed to maturity, so here I'll focus on the basic vegetative methods of reproducing plants. This involves dividing plants or pruning off a variety of different parts of a plant and then encouraging the pieces to grow roots of their own. Once they do, they can be treated like a new plant and cared for as you would the mother plant.

One or more of the basic techniques that follow will suit almost any plant you will ever grow. I've listed some of the more well-known plants that are suitable for each method, but often there are several ways to propagate the same plant. And leaf cuttings, for example, can be prepared in a number of different ways depending on the leaf, so by all means do some research online to find the best method to propagate a particular species if you want to take your plant parenting to the next level.

‘What could be more exciting than creating a new plant, at virtually no cost and in the comfort of your own home?’

How to

DIVIDE PLANTS

One of the easiest ways to create new plants is by division. Some plants grow shoots from underground stems, or rhizomes, and these shoots can be cut from the mother plant to create a new one. Most clumping plants can be divided in this way, and because the baby plant has its own roots already, it has a head start over other forms of propagation – it will quickly establish itself and grow into a mature plant. Plants that can be multiplied using this method include snake plant (*Dracaena trifasciata*), Chinese evergreen (*Aglaonema*), dumb cane (*Dieffenbachia*) and peace lily (*Spathiphyllum*).

YOU WILL NEED:

- Plant with a clumping growth habit
- Sharp knife
- Plastic nursery pot
- Appropriate potting mix for your new plant (see Soil, Pots and Repotting chapter, page 79)

1 Gently remove the plant from the pot.

2 Identify which stems you want to divide from the mother plant. It's preferable to choose sections that have developed their own roots, and then it's as simple as using a sharp knife to cut through the rhizome connecting the plantlet to the main plant.

3 Gently pull the plantlet from the root ball.

4 Pot up the plantlet and there you have it – a new plant ready to be cared for as you would the mother plant. You can cut off as many stems as you like, depending on how many new plants you want to grow.

TIP:
The ideal time to divide plantlets from the mother plant is when you're repotting (see page 98), though it can be done at any time throughout the warmer months.

4

How to

DIVIDE TUBERS, CORMS & BULBS

Some plants grow from swollen, modified underground roots, stems or leaf tissues in which they store water and nutrients. These comprise a number of popular indoor plants, including angel wings (*Caladium*), purple shamrock (*Oxalis triangularis*), cyclamen (*Cyclamen persicum*), tuberous begonia (*Begonia* × *tuberhybrida*), ornamental yam (*Dioscorea discolor*), and amaryllis (*Hippeastrum*). These plants can be propagated by cutting the main tuber or corm into sections and by separating the small bulbils that are produced by the main bulb. This needs to be done when the plant is still dormant and preferably before you replant it just before its growing season.

YOU WILL NEED:

- Plant that grows from a tuber, corm or bulb
- Sharp knife
- Plastic nursery pots
- Core indoor mix (see page 84)

Bulbs that form small bulbils

1 These bulbs are found in plants like amaryllis and purple shamrock. Gently pull the smaller bulbs off the main bulb; if they are firmly attached, cut the bulbils from the main plant instead.

2 Pot these up a few centimetres beneath the surface of the potting mix as you would a mature bulb.

Tubers and corms with multiple 'eyes' or growth buds

1 You'll find tubers in plants such as angel wings and corms in plants like cyclamen. Cut the tuber or corm into pieces with a clean, sharp knife. Make sure each piece has an eye or growth bud (just like a potato) and a good-sized piece of the main tuber or corm.

2 Let the cut areas dry for 24 hours and then plant 3–5 cm below the surface of your potting mix as you would a mature tuber or corm.

How to

GROW FROM OFFSETS PRODUCED ON RUNNERS

Many plants with a sprawling or creeping growth habit – like the Chinese money plant (*Pilea peperomioides*) and alocasias – send out runners: these are long stems that grow underground, called rhizomes, or along the top of the soil, called stolons. The stems develop little offsets or plantlets on the ends. Other plants produce stolons from the crown of the plant, like the spider plant (*Chlorophytum comosum*), on which clusters of offsets form at the tips. These small 'pups', as they are known, can be separated from the parent plant as soon as they have developed a few sets of leaves and roots of their own.

YOU WILL NEED:

- Plant with offsets on runners
- Sharp knife or scissors
- Plastic nursery pot
- Propagation mix (see page 94)

1 Wait until the small 'pups' are at least a few centimetres high and preferably with a vigorous set of new roots – this means they will have enough maturity to support themselves and take off quickly when they are separated.

2 Cut the pups from the stolon or rhizome, being careful not to damage the roots. Trim the stems so that there is only a centimetre or so still attached to each pup.

3 Plant the pups into propagation mix to encourage the roots to grow well.

4 Give them a good water. Once the pups are actively growing, transplant them into a suitable regular potting mix and care for them as you would a mature specimen.

How to

GROW FROM STEM CUTTINGS

Rooting plants from stem cuttings is one of the easiest ways to propagate new plants. This propagation method can be used for both woody and herbaceous plants but you may need to do some research to find out if a particular plant is suitable for this kind of cutting. Some popular indoor plants that you can propagate this way are pothos (*Epipremnum aureum*), arrowhead plant (*Syngonium*), spiderwort (*Tradescantia*), Swiss cheese plant (*Monstera deliciosa*), English ivy (*Hedera helix*), philodendrons and rex begonia vine (*Cissus discolor*).

It's important to choose the right season to strike cuttings. The best time is early spring and throughout summer because this is generally the growth period for most plants: their tissue is full of hormones that will encourage new roots, helping to establish the new plant before the cooler months when many plants go dormant. Taking cuttings in autumn and winter is risky and a larger percentage will fail to strike and instead rot.

YOU WILL NEED:

- Woody or herbaceous plant
- Sharp knife or scissors
- Rooting hormone powder or gel
- Plastic nursery pot
- Propagation mix (see page 94)
- Small stake
- Plastic bag
- Plastic-coated wire garden tie or twine

1

2

3

4

6

5

1 When taking a stem cutting, you need to keep a few things in mind. First, you want to use the current or immediate past season's growth from the top of a plant because older tissue is less likely to strike. Second, avoid stems with flower buds, if possible, and if you can't then remove them from the cutting so they don't drain the energy needed to grow roots. Finally, the terminal end or growing tip of a stem is generally best, though it's possible to use longer shoots cut into several cuttings if you choose. When you have settled on the stems you want to use, prune each off the plant using an angled cut. Each cutting should be a section of healthy plant approximately 10–15 cm long.

TIP:

The morning is the best time to take cuttings because this is when water levels in the stems and leaves are at their highest. If you can't pot up cuttings straight away, park them in a container with a few centimetres of water in a cool, shaded position. They will be fine there for a few days.

2 Prepare the cutting by removing the leaves from the lower half of the cut stem. If a plant has large leaves, cut the remaining ones in half to reduce the stress on the rootless stem – the larger the surface area of the leaves, the more water the cutting will lose through transpiration.

3 Next dip the cut end in the rooting powder or gel to encourage striking. It's not essential to do this but I have found it very effective.

4 Now the cutting is ready to be planted into the propagation mix. Poke a hole into the mix and insert the cutting from a third to about half its length into the pot. If you are propagating multiple cuttings, make sure they aren't too close together: you want to ensure each cutting can get light and air circulation to all its leaves. Water well.

TIP:

Using clear plastic pots to strike cuttings means that you can see the new roots as they make their way through the mix. Not only is it incredibly satisfying to see the cuttings take off but there's no need to disturb them until you're sure they've rooted.

5 Push a small stake into the potting mix and place a plastic bag over the top of the cutting, making sure the bag is large enough to avoid touching the cutting. Use some tie or twine to fasten the bag around the rim of the pot.

6 Place your mini propagation greenhouse in a position with bright indirect light that's warm but not hot, and let nature do its thing. Rooting times will vary from plant to plant and month to month, but once you see some signs of new leaf growth, you can pot up your new plant and treat it as you would your other indoor plants.

TIP:

Place pots of cuttings on top of your tumble drier. The warmth generated when you use it, especially in cooler months, will have a beneficial effect, encouraging root development.

How to

GROW FROM PETIOLE LEAF CUTTINGS

Leaf cuttings are fascinating things. I often wonder why we can't simply cut off a finger, plant it in some high-tech gel and grow another one of us?! While we are far more complex organisms than plants and there are obvious reasons why we can't grow another person from a cutting, it is still wondrous to watch a single leaf take root and then develop little plants around its base. The African violet (*Saintpaulia ionantha*) and ZZ plant (*Zamioculcas zamiifolia*) are perhaps the most well-known plants that can be replicated using this method, but there are a few others that might surprise you, including watermelon peperomia (*Peperomia argyreia*), fiddle-leaf fig (*Ficus lyrata*) and Chinese money plant (*Pilea peperomioides*). Here I'll show you how to grow a plant from petiole leaf cuttings, which consist of the leaf with a petiole (stem) attached.

YOU WILL NEED:

- Plant suitable for petiole leaf cuttings
- Sharp knife or scissors
- Rooting hormone powder or gel
- Plastic nursery pot
- Propagation mix (see page 94)
- Plastic bag
- Plastic-coated wire garden tie or twine

1
2
3
4

1 First you need to remove a healthy leaf cleanly from the plant. Choose one that has matured but isn't older than a year. Some leaves can be gently pulled from the plant, but others will need to be cut off. Allow up to 5 cm of petiole.

2 Dip the cut end into the rooting powder or gel.

3 Insert the lower half of the petiole into propagation mix. Gently compress the mix to keep the leaf firmly in position.

4 Carefully water the plant.

5 Fasten a plastic bag over the top with the tie or twine. Small shoots will develop around the base of the petiole, and these will grow into small plants – sometimes numerous plantlets will develop on a single cutting. Wait until they are at least 2–3 cm high, with roots of their own, before gently pulling or cutting them from the mother leaf for potting up as you would an adult plant.

TIP:

Instead of planting straight into propagation mix, you can strike petiole leaf cuttings using the water method. Fill a jar or glass with water up to 1 cm from the rim and put some aluminium foil over the top. Make holes in the foil where you want the stems to go and push each leaf stem through so that the bottom 2 cm is under water. The foil supports the leaves above the glass, encouraging air circulation, and also keeps the stems from being over-submerged in the water. Change the water once every 2 weeks. When the roots are more than 1 cm long, pot the cuttings up into propagation mix and leave them to grow for a few weeks, before transferring to regular potting mix (water roots are not fully formed so the plants will do better if they spend some time strengthening in propagation mix first).

How to

GROW FROM SECTIONAL LEAF CUTTINGS

Some leaves can be cut into sections and each section will root and sprout small plantlets. Plants suitable for sectional leaf cuttings include rex begonias, snake plant (*Dracaena trifasciata*), felt bush (*Kalanchoe beharensis*) and copper spoons (*Kalanchoe orgyalis*).

YOU WILL NEED:

- A plant suitable for sectional leaf propagation
- A sharp knife or scissors
- Rooting hormone powder or gel
- Plastic nursery pot
- Propagation mix (see page 94)
- Plastic bag
- Plastic-coated wire garden tie or twine

1

2

3

4

5

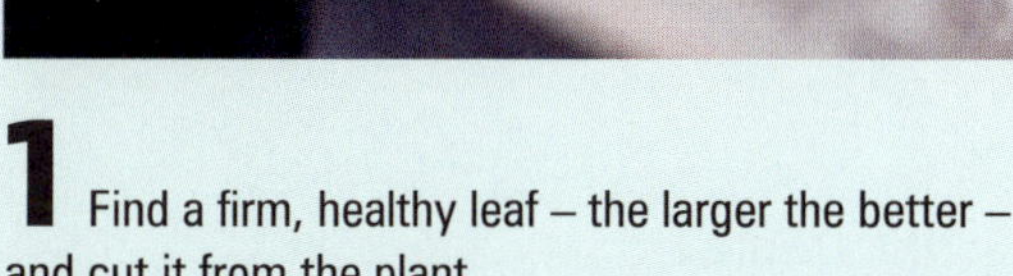

1 Find a firm, healthy leaf – the larger the better – and cut it from the plant.

2 Lay it flat and locate the main leaf veins. Cut the leaf into several wedge-shaped sections, making sure that each contains a main leaf vein running through the centre. If the plant has long, narrow leaves, such as the snake plant, cut the leaf into rectangular sections about 6–10 cm long, as you would cut a stalk of celery into crudités.

3 You should now have a number of sections of leaf. If they are quite long, cut the top half off each one, so that you are left with triangular sections with nice thick veins.

4 Dip the base of each section into the rooting powder or gel.

5 Make small grooves in the propagation mix, deep enough to cover the lower third of each cutting. Place a cutting into each groove. If the leaf sections are top heavy, insert a toothpick behind each section to support and keep it upright.

6 Water the leaf sections carefully.

7 Place a plastic bag over the top and tie to secure. Now wait. Each cutting will root and start to produce small plants around the base of the cut section. Once the plantlets are 1 cm or so high remove the bag so they can adjust to cooler conditions (a process called hardening off). When they are at least a few centimetres high, carefully knock the plants and soil out of the pot, separate the individual new plants and pot them up to be cared for as you would the mother plant.

TIP:

Keep a close eye on cuttings when they are under plastic bags – it's a good idea to remove the bag once a week or so to allow fresh air to circulate. If you notice any cuttings developing a fungal disease or rotting, spray them with an anti-fungal spray immediately and discard any cuttings that have turned soft and brown or have mildew on them.

How to

GROW FROM AIR LAYERING

Air layering involves wrapping a moist material, such as sphagnum moss, around an area of stem with root nodes to induce roots to develop. This is ideal for larger sections of plants, such as the top of a climbing philodendron, and is a great method to use when a single-stemmed climbing plant has aged and lost its lower foliage, leaving an ugly and often elongated bare stem. Plants can also outgrow their homes, becoming specimens many metres high. Plants like these need a revamp to look their best and once the lower section of stem is gone its surprising how new and fresh they will appear. And the good news is that the stem remaining in the old pot will reshoot to become an actively growing plant again. You can use this method for philodendrons, Swiss cheese plant (*Monstera deliciosa*), dragon tail (*Rhaphidophora decursiva*) and pothos (*Epipremnum aureum*). A plant doesn't need to be climbing on a totem to use air layering; rubber plant (*Ficus elastica*), for example, can also be propagated this way.

YOU WILL NEED:

- Long-stemmed plant
- Sharp knife
- Rooting hormone powder or gel
- Plastic nursery pot
- Scissors
- Sticky tape
- Sphagnum moss
- Small stake or chopstick
- Plastic-coated wire garden tie or twine

1
2
3
4
5
6

1 Select the point on the stem where you want the base of the new plant to be and remove any leaves growing from that point. Take a knife and about 5 cm below a leaf node carefully cut approximately halfway through the main stem of the plant – be careful not to cut all the way through. You are doing this to signal to the plant that it needs to develop new roots above the cut to supplement its uptake of water and nutrients.

2 Apply rooting powder or gel to the cut and around the stem where the node is situated.

3 Take your plastic nursery pot and cut it in half lengthways with some scissors.

4 Place the two halves of the plastic pot around the part of the plant you have cut, and tape it together so that it sits securely against the plant.

5 Moisten the sphagnum moss and carefully stuff it into the plastic pot.

6 Use a small stake or chopstick to push the moss down until the pot is full and both the cut and the leaf node are completely covered.

7 Water in well. It's important to keep the moss moist, so ideally wrap the nursery pot with a layer of plastic wrap. Leave the roots to develop until there are a good number of them (this could happen within a month or take up to 6 months, depending on the species and time of year). Remove the plastic wrap from the nursery pot, then remove the pot itself and cut all the way through the stem a centimetre or so below where the bottom of the pot was. Gently tease out as much moss as you can from the delicate new roots, then pot up the new plant in fresh potting mix. Water in well with some diluted seaweed solution and care for the new plant as usual. The lower part of the stem that is still on the mother plant will also reshoot, leaving you with two gorgeous plants instead of one.

THANK YOU

To my family and friends who tell me I'm great even when I'm not, and believe it even when I don't.

To Kent Miller-Randle and Bonny Dixon, thank you for your unconditional love and support.

To Jan Kavanagh, thank you for always having my back and ditto above.

To Nunung, Armang and my Bali family, through you I have discovered you don't need to be related to be family. X

To Jack and Beth Brighton, for your knowledge, friendship and support when it really mattered; RIP.

To the ABC *Gardening Australia* team, thank you for the opportunity to present 'The Great Indoors' and for having faith in me as a TV presenter.

To my followers on Instagram, thank you for your support and feedback, it means the world to me.

To Lena Barridge, my manager, and Henrie Stride Management, thank you for your kindness, faith and wisdom.

Thank you Mark Roper, your generosity, ease and talent made every shoot day a delight and a true collaboration.

To Mary Small, Jane Winning, Praveen Naidoo, Eugenie Baulch and Michelle Mackintosh, patience is a virtue. But you know that because you have just made a book with me. Gratitude is also a virtue and I have buckets of it for each of you. Special thanks to Michelle, who has made my first book so beautiful. X

Thank you to my MRD Home team, I am lucky to have you all and truly appreciate each of you.

Thank you to Collectors Corner, Melbourne, for putting up with me and Mark wandering around snapping pics all day.

Thank you Bella, my pooch, who is simply kindness on four legs.

INDEX

N

O

P

R

Pan Macmillan acknowledges the Traditional Custodians of country throughout Australia and their connections to lands, waters and communities. We pay our respect to Elders past and present and extend that respect to all Aboriginal and Torres Strait Islander peoples today. We honour more than sixty thousand years of storytelling, art and culture.

A Plum book

First published in 2021 by
Pan Macmillan Australia Pty Limited
Level 25, 1 Market Street,
Sydney, NSW, Australia 2000

Level 3, 112 Wellington Parade,
East Melbourne, Victoria, Australia 3002

Design by Michelle Mackintosh
Typesetting by Megan Ellis
Editing by Eugenie Baulch
Index by Helena Holmgren
Photography by Mark Roper and Craig Miller-Randle
Styling by Craig Miller-Randle
Colour reproduction by Splitting Image Colour Studio
Printed and bound in China by 1010 Printing International Limited

A CIP catalogue record for this book is available from the National Library of Australia.

10 9 8 7 6 5 4 3 2 1